SOCIAL STRESS
IN THE UNITED STATES

SOCIAL STRESS IN THE UNITED STATES

Links to Regional Patterns in Crime and Illness

ARNOLD S. LINSKY
MURRAY A. STRAUS
University of New Hampshire

 Auburn House Publishing Company
Dover, Massachusetts

Library of Congress Cataloging in Publication Data
Linsky, Arnold S. (Arnold Stanley)
    Social stress in the United States.

    Bibliography: p.
    Includes index.
    1. Stress (Psychology)—Social aspects—United States.
2. Life change events—United States. 3. Social
adjustment. 4. Social problems. I. Straus, Murray
Arnold, 1926-   . II. Title.
HM291.L49 1986   302   86-14192
ISBN 0-86569-149-5

Printed in the United States of America

FOREWORD

Both scholars and lay people have been attracted to the idea of stress and its role in the etiology of illness and maladaptive behavior. When Norman Scotch and I were preparing to study life stress among subjects in the Framingham Heart Study, we first carried out open-ended interviews with researchers and lay people to learn what specific types of stress they thought might contribute to the development of cardiovascular disease. What impressed us particularly was that the idea of stress was salient to everyone, with each person subscribing to some type of causal model.

When Sydney Croog and I were studying over 400 men who had experienced their first heart attack, we were surprised to learn that an overwhelming proportion of them unhesitatingly attributed their heart attack to stress or worries on the job or in the home. Patients were quick to describe such stressors as having an unsympathetic superior or colleague, excessive work loads, or perennial problems with children. It would seem, then, that the sociologist's task as teacher or investigator of stress is a relatively easy one.

On closer inspection, however, the quick receptivity to the idea of stress displayed by many lay people and behavioral scientists is generally confined to the psychological level. People easily resonate to the importance of such traumatic life events as the death of a spouse or the loss of a job, so well developed and amplified by Holmes and Rahe. But as we move from the personal psychological experience to the larger social-structural realm where the sociologist may make distinctive contributions, the task of conceptualization and instruction becomes more challenging.

The authors point out the limitations in the individualistic emphasis which has characterized much research on stress. They direct our attention to the importance of social organization in generating stress and in influencing responses to stress. They are to

v

be commended for their imaginative effort in exploring the relationship between social structure, and illness and crime. They are also to be commended for their exploitations of secondary data in order to construct a composite stress index for each state in the United States. Because the field of stress research is growing so rapidly, the reader will welcome the effort by the authors to systematize much of the literature and to address some of the conceptual issues in the field.

SOL LEVINE, PH. D.
University Professor and
Professor of Sociology and Public Health
Boston University

ACKNOWLEDGMENTS

The authors were helped by many in completing this research. We benefited from the intelligent and dedicated work of a succession of research assistants, especially Susan Frankel, John Ost, and Kimberly Vogt. Special thanks are due to Dr. John P. Colby, Jr., our collaborator on the stress and alcohol papers, who also performed much of the computer analysis for the book and improved the project with insightful suggestions. Our colleague in the Department of Sociology, Larry Hamilton, enlightened us with several useful discussions on multivariate analysis. Several discussants of early papers from the project at meetings of the American Sociological Association, Eastern Sociological Society, and Society for the Study of Social Problems provided valuable critiques. Sieglinde Fizz, the Administrative Assistant of the Family Research Laboratory, supervised much of the data entry and the typing of numerous revisions. She kept the research from being crowded out by many competing projects. Heidi Gerhard managed the difficult task of creating a seemingly endless number of tables showing the rank order of the states. We are grateful to all of these people. Any shortcomings in the book are ours, not theirs.

We are grateful to the National Institutes of Health for providing funds to the University of New Hampshire Biomedical Research Fund, which supported the work on stress and illness, to the National Institute of Mental Health for grant number T32 MH15161, which supported the work on stress and crime, and to the University of New Hampshire for general support of our research.

ARNOLD S. LINSKY AND MURRAY A. STRAUS
*Department of Sociology and Anthropology, and
Family Research Laboratory, University of New Hampshire*

CONTENTS

Part One

STRESS AND SOCIETY

Chapter 1

A SOCIOLOGICAL PERSPECTIVE ON STRESS

The Social Aspects of Stress

Americans tend to think of "stress" as a "psychological" phenomenon. Part of the reason for this is that a great deal of the research on stress has been done by psychologists and psychiatrists who, quite naturally and appropriately, tend to focus their work on the psychological problems of individual persons. Another reason for seeing stress as an individual psychological phenomenon is the tendency of Americans to "psychologize" almost everything. We are a very individualistically oriented society (Williams, 1970), so it seems "natural" to explain almost any aspect of behavior by referring to variables that are in the makeup of individual persons—that is, to explain things by recourse to psychological variables. Similarly, when we think about the consequences of something like "stress," there is a tendency to focus almost exclusively on the effects of stress for individual persons.

Of course, stress *is* a psychological phenomenon in the sense that it is experienced by individual persons. But there are at least three ways in which it is also a sociological phenomenon.

1. The causes of stress are to be found in the nature of society. The events that place people under stress are, for the most part, a result of how society is organized. For example, a society characterized by high rates of unemployment will be a high stress society. In addition, cultural norms and beliefs to a large extent define what will be considered stressful. In

3

the affluent counterculture years of the 1960s and 1970s, for example, getting promoted to a better job came to be viewed as stressful, whereas getting divorced came to be regarded as less stressful than in years past.

2. How people deal with stress is determined at least as much by social rules and social organization as it is by the personality of the person experiencing a stressful event. In some societies people learn to deal with stress by withdrawal and passivity (Parsons, 1954). In other societies, such as the United States, people tend to respond to stress by aggression. Within any society, different sub-groups tend to respond to stress in different ways. Thus, how one deals with or reacts to stress is, to a considerable extent, a function of the society or part of society in which a person is located.

3. The consequences of stress are not confined to the individual. Both the stressfulness of society and the ways people cope with stress have consequences for the very nature of society itself. The pace of economic activity, for example, is likely to be slower in a society in which people tend to deal with stress by withdrawal and passivity than in a society in which people tend to become aggressive under stress. The crime rate is also likely to be higher than average in the latter type of society.

These three sociological aspects of stress point to the fact that the level of stress found in a society and the way members of a society respond to stress are part of what gives each society and each sector of society its unique flavor. The study described in this book was designed to examine each of these sociological aspects of stress. Such an examination can help to answer a number of important questions about stress and its origins and consequences. Hopefully, it will also provide valuable insights about the way in which American society operates.

In our view, the individualistic focus that has characterized most stress research represents an important limitation. One result of the individualistic focus has been to ignore the full range of potentially interesting and important questions about the social aspects of stress, such as the following:

• Does the risk of stressful events vary by position or location within a society?

- Are there greater risks of stress adhering to some statuses and some locations than others?
- Does the accumulation of stressful events in social systems affect the functioning of those systems as well as the functioning of individual members?
- Do high levels of stressful events in communities impact only those who directly experience those events (such as the divorced or unemployed, etc.) or are there "spill-over" effects upon their less directly impacted neighbors?
- How do social and cultural systems structure the direction of response and adaptation to stressful conditions—for example, do stressful events precipitate violent or antisocial reactions in some types of situations and illness in others?

To help answer questions such as these, we developed a measure called the State Stress Index (SSI). The SSI is intended to compare the stressfulness of life in each of the fifty states of the United States. More importantly, the SSI can also be used to find out what factors are associated with state-to-state differences in stress. These correlations can help to answer questions such as those just raised.

Sociological and Life Events Approaches to Stress

Our research owes its theoretical direction to two separate traditions in the study of human stress—what we will call the "sociological" tradition and the "life-events" tradition.

The Sociological Tradition

A great deal of sociological research has related presumably stressful social situations (broken homes, living or working in a hostile environment, coping with migration, discrepancies between aspirations and opportunities, role conflicts, status inconsistency, social isolation, etc.) with various pathological and other reactions. We will illustrate the nature of this research by summarizing three of the main approaches used by sociologists to study stress.

Social Disorganization. Research stemming from the tradition of the "social disorganization school" (Rubington and Weinberg, 1977) has emphasized the disruptive effects of rapid social change on both individuals and communities, including (1) rural to urban and long-distance migration (Malzburg and Lee, 1956), (2) disruption of intimate ties in urban environments and breakdown of community (Faris and Dunham, 1939), and (3) the consequences of broken homes (Nye, 1958). The dependent variables (presumed effects of stress) in these studies have included crime, mental illness, suicide, family dissolution, and delinquency. Studies with particular relevance for this research include the linkage of rapid social change and the necessity of adaptation to new conditions with development of mental disorders (Fried, 1964; Malzburg and Lee, 1956; Murphy, 1959; and Wechsler, 1961).

Work in this "social disorganization" tradition is extensive (spanning several decades) but diffuse, and for the most part not closely integrated with theory. The writings of this group have not emphasized stress per se as the intervening variable between social disorganization and the various pathologies as much as they have emphasized the breakdown of social control under conditions of social disorganization, which then fails to deter deviance on the part of individuals.

Status and Role Inconsistency.   Another group of studies has focused on consistency between statuses, termed "status crystallization," "status consistency," and so forth. These studies are based on the theory that certain status configurations (combinations of statuses) are more stressful than others. For example, the combination of high ascribed status and low achieved status has been linked to psychosomatic symptoms (Jackson, 1962; Jackson and Burke, 1965).

Gibbs and Martin (1964) developed a complex measure of the degree of "integration" among several statuses that individuals occupy at the same time (e.g., marital, occupational, age group, sex, race, etc). Rarely occupied combinations of these statuses are given low scores on the measure of status integration, and low scores have been found to be highly linked to high rates of suicide and mental illness. Such positions are presumably stressful because individuals occupying these rare status combinations may experience role conflict and may be impeded from forming stable relations with others.

A study by Dodge and Martin, *Social Stress and Chronic Illness: Mortality Patterns in Industrial Society* (1970), uses the same measure of status integration as do Gibbs and Martin. Their measure is directly relevant to the present book. Both Dodge and Martin and our own study focus on stress as the independent variable, and there is an overlap in the set of dependent variables (heart disease and cirrhosis) that are also included in our dependent variables. In addition, at least some of Dodge and Martin's analysis is done with state data (for thirty states). Theirs is a very different study from the one presented here, however.

Although the theory of status integration has been criticized on a number of theoretical and methodological grounds (Chambliss and Steele, 1966; Roghmann, 1972), it successfully predicts variations in suicide rates (Gibbs and Martin, 1964) and mortality from certain chronic illnesses (Dodge and Martin, 1970). However, the merits of the status inconsistency approach to measuring stress are tangential to our research because that measure of stress is quite different—conceptually and methodologically—from the "life events" approach.

Merton's Anomie Theory. Stress may be produced by cultural systems that encourage or prescribe behavior which the social structure does not permit. This has been an important focus in the sociology of social problems for several decades since Robert Merton's classic work on anomie and deviant behavior (1957).

According to Merton, the gulf between the desire and expectation for upward mobility on the one hand (to which most persons are socialized in our culture) and low achievement levels caused by limited opportunities, leads to the breakdown of legitimate norms and ultimately deviant adaptation for some. Others have suggested that such gaps between culturally promoted expectations and opportunities can result in higher rates of violence (Cloward and Ohlin, 1960; Cohen, 1955), schizophrenia (Parker and Kleiner, 1966), and depression (Linsky, 1969).

Limitations of the Sociological Tradition. Despite the important contributions of studies just cited, certain limitations in our opinion require a new approach to sociological research on stress. One of the most important limitations is that generally "stress" has been an imputed but unobserved intervening variable between stressful social situations and pathological outcomes. Measurement of stress in the sociological traditions has ranged from relatively simple comparison of different groups or locations within the social structure (e.g., family status, social class, neighborhood, mobility status, etc.), some of which are presumed in the literature to be more stressful than others (Levine and Scotch, 1970), to elaborate quantitative measures such as Gibbs and Martin's measure of status integration (1964) just discussed or Parker

and Kleiner's measure of goal-striving stress (1966). More generally, the diffuseness of the stress concept in the sociological literature limits its usefulness and in some ways makes it almost
synonymous with the sociology of social problems.

The Life Events Tradition

Much of the recent interest in stress stems from work in psychosomatic medicine, which has sought linkage between stressful
changes in the lives of individuals and the onset of illness or other
debilities. A major stimulus to this research occurred with the
publication in 1967 by Holmes and Rahe of the "Social Readjustment Rating Scale." The scale contains forty-three items, each
listing a "life change event," intended to represent fairly common
albeit stressful events, such as getting married, getting divorced,
birth of a child, death of a child, moving to a new house, losing a
job, getting promoted, and so forth. Respondents indicate if any of
the "life events" have recently occurred. What all events have in
common is that they are presumed to require important changes in
ongoing adjustment—that is, they make certain demands for readjustment on the person experiencing the event. The scale includes
items that are both positively valued in American society, such as
marriage, births, and significant personal achievements, as well as
events that are negatively valued or undesirable, such as divorce or
death.

The theory behind the Social Readjustment Rating Scale (and
the other "life events" indexes that have appeared since then) is
that each of these events involves a certain adaptive demand. If
several life events occur simultaneously or within a limited period
of time, they may impose demands that exceed the ability of the
individual to cope. This, in turn, will be subjectively experienced
as stress and will manifest itself in illness and other maladaptive
behavior.

Holmes and his associates found support for the hypothesis that
the amount of social readjustment required by life events is an
important causal factor in the incidence of illness (Holmes and
Masuda, 1974). For example, they found that individuals experiencing more than 300 "life-change" units (obtained by totaling the
weighted score for each event experienced) in the course of a year's
time were more than twice as likely to be physically ill within the
following year as persons having less than 200 units of change.

Similarly, the higher the total "life-change" score, the more severe the illness was likely to be (Wyler, Masuda, and Holmes, 1968).

Other researchers report finding that a high number of events serves as a precipitator that determines the timing but not the type of illness (Rabkin and Streuning, 1976) and that life events scores are also correlated with development of psychiatric disorders, depressed mood, imprisonment, and pregnancy among others (Dohrenwend and Dohrenwend, 1974).

Criticisms of Life Events Research. Literally scores of studies have now replicated the relationship between accumulation of stressful events and illness. To be sure, correlations are low, but the basic relationship is stable, and at least some of the studies use a prospective design. Certainly, many issues remain to be resolved, including those that concern the process by which stressful events are linked to illness and disorders—that is, the sociological, psychological, and behavioral processes that intervene between life change and illness. There are also methodological problems of how life events should be selected and combined within scales, who should judge the stressfulness of events, whether so-called "positive" events are really stressful, and how to determine the scope of stress-related adaptation for which the life events scales have predictive powers.

Some of these issues are dealt with in later chapters. However, two of the criticisms of life events research need to be considered at this point. One of the most important is Thoits's conclusion (1981) that the previously well established correlations between undesirable life events and disease may have been inflated due to inclusion of health-related items in the life events checklists. Thus there is a potential confounding of the independent and dependent variables. Thoits therefore urges those investigating the relationship between life events and physical illness to use a version of the life events checklist that does not contain health-related events (Thoits, 1981:107). Fortunately, our study is not vulnerable to this problem. We excluded from the stress index indicators of illness, accidents, deaths, and involvement in the criminal justice system to avoid the possibility of such circularity.

Another criticism is whether life events research has shown relationships with illness per se or with "sick role" or care-seeking behavior, since medical care is often used as the operational definition of illness (Mechanic, 1974). Many earlier studies are unclear in determining whether the results of life events are an increase in illness or only an increase in "illness behavior." Complaining and seeking medical advice can increase the chances of a case being identified (Kasl and Cobb, 1966). Those experiencing stressful life situations may be likely to perceive their health as poor, report medical symptoms, and seek medical assistance (Mechanic, 1974). We deal with this issue mainly by using death rates as the indicators of illness rather than treatment data.

Limitations of the Life Events Tradition.   From the perspective of sociology, the obvious limitation of the life events tradition is that it has focused almost exclusively on the individual level rather than on the social system level of analysis. The main exception is studies that use economic change as the independent variable (Brenner, 1980a; Dooley and Catalano, 1980; Eyer, 1977a,b) and studies by Farrington and Linsky (1976) and Farrington (1980b).

The Farrington and Linsky research considered a broad range of critical life events at the social system level. For example, Farrington and Linsky aggregated items from the Holmes-Rahe "Schedule of Recent Life Events" for the state of New Hampshire. They found that monthly increases in aggregated life events correspond with increases in admissions to outpatient community mental health centers throughout the state, with approximately a four-month time lag. For the United States as a whole, Farrington (1980b) also found that changes in aggregated life events were related with various time lags to changes in rates of sick role behavior, suicide, and illness over a 132-consecutive-month period. Both of these studies were important in the development of the research described in this book because they demonstrate the feasibility of transforming life events research to the level of the social system. In fact, it was the discovery of this possibility that first attracted us to conduct research on social stress.

Integrating the Two Traditions

An interesting phenomenon from the standpoint of the sociology of science is that those working in the "life events" approach to stress and those working in the "status integration" approach (who also claim to be examining social stress) appear to have little or no impact on one another. For example, Dodge and Martin (1970) make no reference to any of the life events studies, and we found only one passing reference to Dodge and Martin in a large sample of life events articles in our files.

We think that much is to be gained by integrating the life events and the various sociological perspectives on stress. Consequently, our research draws on these traditions. It translates the life events approach from the individual level to the level of the social system so that the stressfulness of living in various geographic units, such as states and regions of the United States, can be evaluated. It also lets us investigate the relation of geographic variations in social stress to a number of dependent variables—variables that are widely believed to be linked to stress, such as certain illnesses, alcohol addiction, and crime and violence.

Both the sociological and the life events traditions have made important contributions to understanding stress, and both have important limitations. By adapting the life events approach to the study of stress in social systems, we hope to incorporate at least some of the advantages of both traditions.

Theoretical and Practical Importance of Research on Social Stress

Theoretical Issues

There is evidence that stress in general, and in particular stressful life events, exacts a toll in physical disease, mental illness, and other types of disorders (Dohrenwend and Dohrenwend, 1974; Dooley and Catalano, 1980). However, as mentioned earlier, that research has been restricted almost exclusively to the individual as the unit of analysis (see Catalano and Dooley, 1977; Farrington and Linsky, 1976; and Farrington, 1980b, for exceptions). Such research links life changes *for individuals* with the onset of illness and other problems.

Stress as a Social System Property. In our view, this individualistic bias, owing perhaps to its clinical origins in psychosomatic research, represents an important limitation of life events research. The theoretical approach of the research to be reported in this book assumes that some locations in the social system are more stressful than others. More specifically, we intend to test the theory that stressful events which vitally affect individuals are component processes of the social system itself. They are structured and vary across such systems and conform to patterns of relationship that may not be predictable from knowledge about the individuals. Part of this study then deals with how stressor events are broadly patterned and distributed across social structures through examining state-by-state variations in stressful events as measured by the State Stress Index (SSI) described in Chapter 2.

Societal Stress, Crime, Maladaptive Behavior, and Disease. The major part of the study is concerned with understanding the link between the stressfulness of social systems, and crime and other maladaptive behaviors. Our general hypothesis is that *the higher the level of social stress, the higher the level of health problems and crime*. However, the contributions we hope to make are more general and also more subtle than merely establishing whether there is a correlation between the SSI and the indicators of crime and maladaptive behavior, important as that is. At the most general level, we began the study in the belief that it could increase understanding of the interrelationships between social structure and individual well-being. In part this is because the study investigates a number of complex interrelationships among the variables, including curvilinear and interactive relationships.

Curvilinear Relationships. A previous research study using individual level data (Straus, 1980b) examined the link between stress and physical aggression between spouses. That study found relatively little association between scores on the stress index and marital violence until the level of stress reached about one standard deviation above the mean. Thereafter, each successive point on the stress index was associated with a large increase in the assault rate. Straus interpreted this finding as indicating that individuals can withstand a considerable number of stress-producing changes in their lives without difficulty, but that there is a threshold, after which successful coping becomes more and more problematic. Since an exponential function of this type might also be found at the social system level, we used the Breakdown program of SCSS to test for non-linearity and to examine the plots for such non-linear relationships. Several significant deviations from linearity were found, but inspection of the plots did not reveal any that approximated an exponential function or other discernible function.

Sociocultural Factors Affecting the Response to Stress. We also assumed that the link between societal stress and crime and maladaptive behavior is influenced by many other variables. Let us consider the hypothesized association between stress and alcoholism. We do not argue that stress directly causes alcoholism. Alcoholism is only one of many possible responses to stress (see Coleman and Straus, 1983). Among the alternatives are violence, passivity, resignation, flight, or suicide. The absence of a necessary link between stress and particular outcomes is shown by Brenner's data on the correlates of unemployment (1976, 1980a). His time series data show that unemployment is highly correlated with assault and homicide. Brenner also found that unemployment is correlated with alcoholism, hypertension, deaths from heart attacks, and mental hospital admissions. Similarly, Brown and Harris (1978) demonstrated a clear tendency among a sample of women in London to respond to stress by depression.

We believe that one of the variables that determines whether the response to stress will take the form of alcohol abuse or be expressed in some other direction is the presence of a cultural tradition that provides members of that society with the opportunity to learn such patterns and that provides a culturally transmitted script for each type of response to stress. To empirically investigate this issue, we developed and used an index to measure state-to-state differences in the acceptability of alcohol as a means for relieving stress, and state-to-state differences in the legitimacy of violence. In a later chapter we investigate the effects of these aspects of a state's cultural context on the link between stress and alcoholism and violence.

Buffering Variables. We have argued that different social systems generate different amounts of stress and that they structure response to that stress in alternative directions. There are still further ways in which social structures affect stress and its outcome. One of these is the interaction of stressor events with other variables that can mitigate or change the relationship. We therefore examined the buffering effects of selected economic and social resources on the impact of stress. The five buffering variables employed in this study were family integration, political integration, mental health support systems, educational resources, and public assistance generosity. Each was seen as having a potential buffering effect in terms of helping individuals and families cope with stressful events. In Chapters 4 and 5 we examine the impact of these community resources in softening the effects of stress on the community.

Practical Contributions

A considerable amount is known about how the states and regions of the United States differ in political patterns, economic well-being, and various aspects of culture, but there is less systematic knowledge on regional and state differences in social well-being, including stressfulness of the environment (Smith, 1973). The State Stress Index and the rates for various indicators of mental illness and crime developed for this research provide such information for each state and region of the United States. We believe that this information will have potential for application to mental health prevention programs by pinpointing particularly stressful locales for various levels of intervention. For example, primary prevention might involve community attention to the types of "life events" and other structural variables that may be identified in this study as stress-producing.

On the secondary and tertiary prevention levels, it could be helpful to anticipate the direction that stress will take for different locales (for example, inward as in alcoholism, illness, and suicide; or outward in the forms of assaults, murder, delinquency, family violence, etc.). Communities could then direct prevention programs in appropriate directions, such as delinquency prevention programs or parent education, and better plan for distribution of services for those who manifest problems associated with stress, such as alcoholism and mental health treatment services.

Methodological Contributions

The State Stress Index for each state and the rates for various indicators of illness and crime are given in the text or appendix to this book so that these data can be available to other researchers. The SSI, for example, may be useful to researchers who are interested in the relationship of stressful social situations to other consequences of stress not included in the current study. Conversely, the rates of criminal and maladaptive behaviors may be useful to those interested in research designed to test other explanations for these phenomena. But the most promising contribution might come from considering the State Stress Index as a "social indicator." If this measure were to be computed for a series of years, it might provide valuable insights into trends in American society. It would also permit future researchers to use "time series" techniques of data analysis—procedures which are much more powerful than the techniques that we could use because our data are limited to a single year.

Chapter 2

MEASUREMENT OF
SOCIAL SYSTEM STRESS

This chapter describes the development of an index for measuring the stressfulness of life in geographic areas. This index, which we call the "State Stress Index" and will abbreviate as SSI, reflects the frequency of various events included in so-called stressful life events scales. These are events that require major adaptation on the part of residents.

As explained in Chapter 1, the theory underlying the State Stress Index is that the more stressful events occur simultaneously or in close succession, the greater the chance that the resulting adaptive demands will exceed the capacity of people to deal with the necessary adaptations; this outcome will be experienced as stress. The State Stress Index described in this chapter enables the social system aspect, which is implicit in this theory, to be investigated by measuring the extent to which there are state-to-state differences in such stressful events. Or putting it another way, the SSI provides data on whether the residents of each state have a differential risk of experiencing multiple stressor events.

Stress as a Multidimensional Concept

There has been a long debate on the concept of stress and its definition (Lazarus, 1966; McGrath, 1970; Mechanic, 1962; Scott and Howard, 1970; Selye, 1966). For example, one issue is whether stress is a property of the situation (such as illness, unemployment, family conflict, getting married, or getting promoted to a new job) or whether it is a subjective experience. But

15

the situation is much more complex than that suggested by these two aspects. Farrington (1980a) identified six components that need to be measured for research on stress: the stressor stimulus, objective demands, subjective demands, response capabilities, choice of response, and stress level.

Our view of stress can be summarized by saying that it is a function of the interaction of the occurrence of potentially stressful events, subjectively defined demands of a situation, and the capabilities of an individual or group to respond to these demands. Stress exists when the subjectively experienced demands exceed response capabilities. However, the aspect of stress that is measured in this study is limited to the extent to which "stressor events" occur in a social system.

The data we have available permit us to test a number of issues, including some of the processes said to intervene between the experience of stressful life events and the occurrence of maladaptive behavior. For example, we can test the idea that certain social conditions can serve as "buffers" in insulating people from adversely responding to stress. On the other hand, we do not have data in our own study that could be used to determine the extent to which stressor events are subjectively experienced as stressful. Consequently, that part of the theory must remain an assumption. However, there is ample evidence from previous studies by Holmes and Rahe (1967) and others (Dohrenwend and Dohrenwend, 1974) that such events are generally experienced as stressful.

Four other aspects of the theory, within the context of this research, are assumptions, even though each has been studied empirically by others. In fact, there is considerable empirical support for all four. But since they require data unavailable to us, they remain assumptions and therefore need to be called to the attention of readers. The four assumptions are as follows:

1. Some life events, such as moving, produce a certain but unknown degree of demand for adaptation.
2. On the average, these events are subjectively experienced as a demand.
3. The capability of responding to these demands will not always be sufficient.
4. The discrepancy between the situational demands and re-

sponse capabilities will be subjectively experienced as stress-ful.

On the basis of these assumptions, it is then possible to investi-gate the relationship between stressful "life events" and the level of illness, violence, and other maladaptive behavior said to result from stress.

Development of the State Stress Index (SSI)

The research began with a series of pilot studies in which we explored a varied set of indicators of stressful events and a variety of ways of combining these events into a composite index. The first issue that needs to be addressed is the appropriateness of using a composite index such as the SSI as compared with investigating each of the stressful events separately.

Importance of a Composite Index

There are both theoretical and methodological reasons for our decision to give primary attention to a composite index of stressor events.

The Accumulation Theory. The main theoretical reason for using a composite index is that, according to the life events theory of stress, it is not so much the unique quality of any single event but the *cumulation* of several stressful life events within a rela-tively short time span that results in an adjustment overload, eventuating in serious problems for at least some of those experi-encing this overload.

The life events theory of stress, as pointed out earlier, devel-oped out of clinical experience and systematic research at the individual level. Whether it also applies at the social level is the empirical question that was tested in this research. This test requires a composite index to encompass the cumulative part of the theory.

Statistical Advantages of Composite Indexes. A variable of state-to-state differences in the stressfulness of life is an example of a "latent" or "unmeasured" variable, which is operationalized by use of multiple indicators. The use of a multiple-indicator measure decreases dependence on any single indicator, such as unemployment, migration, or divorce, that has been used by some previous investigators as their measure of stress or social disorganization (Brenner, 1973, 1976; Catalano, Dooley, and Jackson, 1981). Single indicators are more easily subject to be interpreted as measuring something other than stress than are multiple indicators. For example, unemployment may also be an indicator of economic well-being, and divorce may be an indicator of diminished social support. That risk, it seems, is much lower when using fifteen varied indicators as we do here since it would be hard to find a common element that all fifteen share beyond the stress of the demands for new adaptation.

Analysis of Individual Events. In addition to examining the theoretical and methodological advantages of a composite stress index, we also believe it is important to examine each of the stressor events included in the SSI. We did this to answer questions such as whether certain events are more important stressors than others or more important in relation to certain dependent variables. We also did analyses involving individual events to find out if the relationship of the SSI to crime and illness is due to the effect of a specific and powerful variable such as unemployment.

Life Events Indicators

One of the objectives of this research was to apply the life events tradition of stress research to the social system level of analysis. Accordingly, we began our search for system-level indicators by reviewing various life events scales. One of the most extensive of the currently available life events scales is the PERI scale developed by B. S. Dohrenwend et al. (1978). There is a high overlap of items between the forty-three items in the original Holmes and Rahe scale and other life events scales, including the PERI.

We decided to use the PERI as the starting point for developing our macro-level scale because it has an extensive list of life events (102), because the events are described with less ambiguity than is the case with the broader categories in the Holmes/Rahe scale, and because the PERI list of events was derived empirically. We attempted to locate a "macro-level" indicator for as many items as possible from the Dohrenwend scale.

Many of the items in the individual level life events scales have direct analogs at the societal level (e.g., "Having an abortion" and the abortion rate; "Built a home," and new housing units authorized per 1,000; and "Lost a home through fire or flood," and families receiving disaster assistance per 100,000). For other events, the state-level indicators only approximate the events in question. Table 2–1 illustrates how some of the individual items from two sections of the Dohrenwend scale are measured at the state level.

Events with No Comparable Macro-Level Indicator. A number of the PERI items cannot be operationalized at the macro level. These include types of events or stressful conditions for which no systematic public data are collected because they are not considered of sufficient public importance, they are too private, or they are not observable. These include items such as "Had trouble with a boss," "Found out that he/she was *not* going to be promoted," "Increased church or synagogue, club, neighborhood or other organizational activities," "Took up a new hobby," "Started a love affair," "Relations with spouse changed for the better," "Marital infidelity," "Trouble with in-laws."

Events in the State Stress Index. Although no macro-level indicator exists for certain of the PERI items, we were able to locate a substantial number that are directly comparable to the individual life events in the PERI scale. The next step was to construct preliminary versions of the State Stress Index and conduct pilot studies exploring these versions of the index. On the basis of the pilot study results (described below), the annual incidence rates for the fifteen stressor events shown in Table 2–2 were selected for inclusion in the State Stress Index.

Weighting. In most life events scales, each event is weighted according to the consensus of judges concerning how much adjustment that event or change requires on average. The present study departs from that procedure in favor of giving each event a weight of one. This was accomplished by transforming all indicators to Z scores before combining them into the SSI.[1]

There are several reasons for equal item weights. It is not clear from previous psychometric studies that scales composed of weighted items produce either very different or superior results than scales in which all items are weighted equally (Nunnally, 1978:296; Straus and Kumagai, n.d.). Some comparisons of weighted and unweighted life events scales (Brown, 1974; Theorell, 1974) find no difference between weighted and unweighted versions, and some find small differences. Although on

PERI Item Number	SSI Macro Indicator	Source
HAVING CHILDREN		
43. Abortion	Legal abortions per 1,000 population, 1977	Statistical Abstract of the U.S.
44. Miscarriage or stillbirth	Fetal deaths per 1,000 live births, 1976	Vital Statistics of the U.S.
45. Found out cannot have children	None	--
46. Child died	Infant deaths per 1,000 live births, 1976	Vital Statistics of the U.S.
RESIDENCE		
55. Moved to better residence or neighborhood		
56. Moved to worse residence or neighborhood	% of population aged 14 + residing in states <= 5 years, 1976	Spring, 1976, Census Report
57. Moved to residence or neighborhood no better or worse than previous one		
58. Unable to move after expecting to be able to		
59. Built a home or had one built	New housing units authorized per 100,000 pop, 1976	Statistical Abstract of the U.S.
60. Remodeled a home	None	--
61. Lost a home through fire, flood or other disaster	Disaster assistance per 100,000 families, 1976	American National Red Cross

Table 2-1 Sample Items from the PERI Scale and SSI Macro Indicators.

Variable Name	Variable
	Economic Stressors
v382r	Business failures per 1 million population, 1976
v452r	Initial unemployment claims per 100,000 adults, 1976
t58r	Workers involved in work stoppages per 100,000 adults, 1975
t183r	Bankruptcy cases commenced per 100,000 adults, 1975
t200r	Mortgage loans foreclosed per 100,000 population, 1976
	Family Stressors
t57	Divorces per 1,000 population, 1976
z120rl	Abortions per 100,000 population, 1977
t207r	Illegitimate live births per 1,000 population aged 14+, 1976
t70r	Infant deaths per 1,000 live births, 1976
t64r	Fetal deaths per 1,000 live births, 1976
	Other Stressful Events
t187r2	Disaster assistance to families by Red Cross per 100,000 population, 1976
p168	% of population aged 14+ residing in state <= 5 yr., 1976
v356r	New housing units authorized per 100,000 population, 1976
t191r2	New welfare recipients per 100,00 population, 1976
t182r	High-school dropouts per 100,00 population, 1976

[a]The data source for each variable is given in Appendix.

Table 2-2   Life Event Indicators in the SSI.

balance there seems to be a small advantage to weighting life events scale items (Dohrenwend et al.:205), we decided against this because the use of weights for the aggregate number of events occurring in communities seems somewhat remote from the conditions and rationale under which the weights were originally derived. Overall, the potential gain did not seem worth the risk of a more complex measure. Further, since the State Stress Index includes some items that are analogous rather than identical to items in the Dohrenwend scale, it seemed unwise to assume that the weights assigned by Dohrenwend's judges apply to those items.

Referent Year for Stress Index

Because society is constantly changing, the older the data used in sociological research, the less confidence that one can have that the findings still hold by the time the research is completed. Consequently, unless one is interested in the circumstances of a particular historical period, it is usually desirable to base a study such as this on the most recent data as possible. This turned out to be 1976. The factors that led to choosing 1976 as the referent year include the following:

1. Many important data series do not become available until some time after the year to which they refer. This is most clearly the case with the vital statistics, where the publication lag is four years. Similar time lags apply to much of the other data.
2. The data for the SSI had to be at least one year earlier than the data for the dependent variables in order to meet the "time order" criterion necessary for cross-lagged panel analysis.
3. The existence of the 1976 "Survey of Income and Education" (conducted by the Bureau of the Census under a congressional mandate) played a critical role in the decision. Were it not for that data set, it would have been necessary to use 1970 as the referent year because, at the time this work was begun in the spring of 1980, the only other source of much of the data needed for the SSI was the 1970 census.

The fact that the 1980 census was in progress at the very time we decided to use 1976 as the referent year made the problem and the basis for the decision particularly clear. Correspondence with the Census Bureau indicated that the needed data would not be available until 1982 or 1983. That might be worth waiting for. Unfortunately, the real delay would have been five years rather than two. This is because the vital statistics data needed to make 1980 the referent year for the State Stress Index do not become available until 1984, and the vital statistics data needed for some of the dependent variables would not be available until 1985.

Pilot Study Versions of the SSI

Special Versions for Health and for Crime Analyses

An important theoretical and methodological problem in research on stress concerns the "dual role" of illness and crime. These may be both reactions to earlier stressful events and also stressors in their own right. Of the 102 items in the Dohrenwend et al. PERI scale, 4 are indicators of health and 13 are indicators of crime and legal matters. If such events were used in the SSI, it could lead to spuriously high correlations between the SSI and most of our dependent variables (Thoits, 1981). Consequently, the first preliminary version of the SSI (Linsky and Straus, 1981) dealt with the dual role of such variables by excluding indicators of illness and crime, even though several of them are operationalizable with state level data.

Although this approach avoids the methodological problem of confounding the independent and dependent variables, it has an important theoretical disadvantage. It ignores the fact that events such as hospitalization and arrest or imprisonment are also important stressors in the lives of individuals and communities. Excluding them could constitute a loss of important information for the SSI. Consequently, in the second pilot study we used a procedure that was designed to avoid both the loss of information inherent in excluding illness and crime as stressors and also to avoid the confounding that occurs if they are included.

To deal with this problem, we constructed different versions or forms of the SSI. "Form H" was used to relate stress to health variables. This version therefore did not include any health-related variables. "Form C," on the other hand, did include health variables but excluded crime and imprisonment data because it was to be used in analyses where crime and prison rates are the dependent variables. The alternate versions of the SSI were intended to recognize the fact that events such as hospitalization or arrest for a crime are stressors as well as possible responses to stress. They permitted us to include data on important sources of stress in the SSI, while avoiding the problem of confounding the independent and dependent variables.

The pros and cons of constructing such alternate forms of the SSI turned out to be a moot point. After constructing these two versions, a methodological analysis revealed that the version of the SSI without either crime or illness indicators was as highly correlated with the dependent variables as were the versions that included illness and crime variables. We therefore decided to avoid the methodological and conceptual complication of working with three stress indexes by using only the version of the SSI that excludes both illness and crime data. The resulting SSI consists of annual incidence rates for fifteen stressor events, as shown in Table 2–2. The source for each of these items is given in the appendix.

Subscales for "Positive" and "Negative" Events

Several critics of the original Holmes/Rahe "Schedule of Recent Life Experience" have suggested that negatively valued life events impact more severely on physical and mental health than positively evaluated events (Rabkin and Streuning, 1976). This suggestion is counter to Holmes and Rahe's contention that all events that require important adaptation exert stress on individuals in proportion to the number of events and the magnitude of the adaptation required. Evidence pro and con from individual correlations has not been conclusive. It appears that negative events may exact a greater toll than positive, but some research shows that positive events are also correlated with physical and mental illness (Gersten et al., 1974).

Because of the controversy concerning positive and negative events, we carried out a pilot study to explore this issue. The pilot study research included separate measures of positive, negative, and ambiguous events. (An ambiguous event is one in which the cultural evaluation is not clearly positive or negative but depends on other circumstances.) Thus there were three scales of stressor events. We examined the correlation of these three indexes with a variety of dependent variables. The results of these pilot studies showed only weak and inconsistent correlations between the positive events index and various dependent variables, in contrast to the strong and consistent correlations found for the negative events index (Linsky and Straus, 1981). The final SSI was therefore revised to exclude the positive events and one of the ambiguous events that we judged to be inappropriate.

Reliability of the SSI

Item Analysis and Factor Structure

Item Analysis. The life events theory of stress does not assume that stressor events are correlated with each other. Moreover, the events deliberately cover as many different spheres of life as possible. Consequently, the only events for which there is any reason to expect to find significant interrelationships are those that deal with the same sphere of life activities, such as family or employment. Thus, neither a traditional item analysis nor a factor analysis is appropriate criteria for the legitimacy of combining these indicators into a summary stressor events index. However, even though there is no theoretical or methodological reason to expect or require that the items in the SSI be correlated with each other, this does not mean that they are not correlated. That is an empirical issue which is addressed in Tables 2–3 and 2–4.

As expected on the basis of the deliberate diversity of the events selected for inclusion in the SSI, the correlations shown in Table 2–3 are mostly non-significant (about two-thirds). There are, however, a number of positive, even though non-significant, correlations in Table 2–3. We therefore used the reliability program in SPSS to do an internal consistency item analysis. The resulting *alpha* coefficient of .63 and the correlations of each of the events with the total State Stress Index (after correcting for the part-whole problem) indicate that there is at least a certain degree of internal consistency in respect to these events—that is, there is a slight tendency for states that are high on one or more of these items to be high on others.

Factor Analysis. Inspection of the correlations in Table 2–3 also suggests some clusters of events. For example, the family-related items of illegitimacy, divorce, abortion, fetal and infant deaths, and new houses have substantial interrelations. But these are not correlated with the economic events such as unemployment, welfare, and strikes. Since the inter-item correlations sug-

Correlation Coefficient

Stressful Events	1	2	3	4	5	6	7	8
1. Business failures per 1M pop	1.00	.29*	.05	.09	.14	.10	.46***	-.10
2. Emplmt securty: Inital claims, @100K adlt pop	.29*	1.00	.28*	-.03	.02	.12	.28*	-.05
3. Work stops, workers involved 100K adult pop	.05	.28*	1.00	.26*	-.08	.12	-.02	-.07
4. Bankruptcy case commenced @ 100K 76 pop	.09	-.03	.26*	1.00	.23	.48***	.04	.00
5. Mortgage loans foreclosed per 100K	.14	.02	-.08	.23	1.00	.30*	.19	.57***
6. Divorces per 1K population	.10	.12	.12	.48***	.30*	1.00	-.04	.08
7. Number of abortions per 100K pop	.46***	.28*	-.02	.04	.19	-.04	1.00	.02
8. Total illegitimate live births @ 1K pop 14+	-.10	.05	-.07	.00	.57***	.08	.02	1.00
9. Infant deaths per 1K live births	-.19	-.24*	.07	-.01	.27*	.05	-.27*	.71***
10. Fetal deaths per 1K live births: total	-.37**	-.21	-.07	-.04	.37**	-.12	.07	.59***
11. Disaster assistance: # families per 100K	.32*	-.03	.11	.15	-.05	-.07	.11	.12
12. Pop 14+ years: % live in state 5 year or less	.07	.13	-.02	.21	.22	.71***	.20	-.08
13. Income: personal: % increase in rate	-.14	-.01	.25*	.20	-.06	.37**	-.29*	.20
14. New welfare recipients per 100K	.23	.36**	.18	.19	.04	.09	.37**	-.13
15. High school dropouts per 100K: estimate	-.25*	.11	.06	-.15	.31*	-.01	-.05	.75***

*=p<.05, **=p<.01, ***=p<.001

Table 2-3   Intercorrelation of Stressful Event Indicators (N = 50).

Stressful Events	Correlation Coefficient						
	9	10	11	12	13	14	15
1. Business failures per 1M pop	-.19	-.37**	.32*	.07	-.14	.23	-.25*
2. Emplmt security: Inital claims, @100K adlt pop	-.24*	-.21	-.03	.13	-.01	.36**	.11
3. Work stops, workers involved 100K adult pop	.07	-.07	.11	-.02	.25*	.18	.06
4. Bankruptcy case commenced @ 100K 76 pop	-.01	-.04	.15	.21	.20	.19	-.15
5. Mortgage loans foreclosed per 100K	.27*	.37**	-.05	.22	-.06	.04	.31*
6. Divorces per 1K population	.05	-.12	-.07	.71***	.37**	.09	-.01
7. Number of abortions per 100K pop	-.27*	.07	.11	.20	-.29*	.37**	-.05
8. Total illegitimate live births @ 1K pop 14+	.71***	.59***	.12	-.08	.20	-.13	.75***
9. Infant deaths per 1K live births	1.00	.54***	.22	-.16	.35**	-.31*	.62***
10. Fetal deaths per 1K live births: total	.54***	1.00	.13	-.22	.10	-.08	.57***
11. Disaster assistance: # families per 100K	.22	.13	1.00	-.24*	.03	-.11	.04
12. Pop 14+ years: % live in state 5 year or less	-.16	-.22	-.24*	1.00	.23	-.01	-.18
13. Income: personal: % increase in rate	.35**	.10	.03	.23	1.00	-.07	.29*
14. New welfare recipients per 100K	-.31*	-.08	-.11	-.01	-.07	1.00	-.04
15. High school dropouts per 100K: estimate	.62***	.57***	.04	-.18	.29*	-.04	1.00

*=p<.05, **=p<.01, ***=p<.001

Table 2-3 Intercorrelation of Stressful Event Indicators (N = 50) (Continued).

Stressor Events	Unrotated Factor Loadings					Communalities
	Fac 1	Fac 2	Fac 3	Fac 4	Fac 5	
1. Business failures per 1M pop	-.39	.36	.50	.12	.39	.69
2. Emplmt security: Inital claims, @100K adlt pop	-.26	.39	.36	.25	-.50	.66
3. Work stops, workers involved 100K adult pop	-.04	.32	-.05	.71	-.21	.66
4. Bankruptcy case commenced @100K 76 pop	-.05	.59	-.20	.20	.33	.54
5. Mortgage loans foreclosed per 100K	.43	.51	.27	-.44	.12	.72
6. Divorces per 1K population	.00	.80	-.43	-.13	.09	.85
7. Number of abortions per 100K pop	-.25	.34	.69	-.20	.03	.70
8. Total illegitimate live births @ 1K pop 14+	.86	.23	.25	-.11	.00	.86
9. Infant deaths per 1K live births	.86	.04	-.05	.17	.14	.79
10. Fetal deaths per 1K live births: total	.77	-.05	.24	-.10	-.05	.66
11. Disaster assistance: # families per 100K	.14	.02	.31	.50	.66	.80
12. Pop 14+ years: % live in state 5 year or less	-.20	.66	-.38	-.41	-.02	.78
13. Income: personal: % increase in rate	.35	.35	-.51	.39	-.12	.66
14. New welfare recipients per 100K	-.32	.36	.40	.14	-.40	.57
15. High school dropout per 100K: estimate	.81	.11	.21	.09	-.34	.83
Eigenvalues	3.46	2.49	1.96	1.51	1.32	
% Variance	23.08	16.61	13.10	10.09	8.81	
Cum % Variance	23.08	39.69	52.79	62.88	71.68	

Table 2-4   Factor Analysis of Stressor Events in the SSI.

gest certain clusters of the items in the SSI, a factor analysis was carried out using the SCSS factor analysis program and the principal components and varimax rotation options. Five factors were extracted, as shown in Table 2–4.

The fact that there are five factors in this set of fifteen items is further indication of the heterogeneity of the events included in the SSI. Moreover, even the first factor is not very strong since it accounts for only 23 percent of the variance in these items.

Since the fourth and fifth factors each accounted for less then 10 percent of the variance in the set of items, we will attempt to interpret only the first three factors. Inspecting the items with high loadings (.5 or over) on the first factor indicates that it is composed of events which have a familial component (illegitimacy, fetal deaths, high school drop-outs, infant deaths, and new housing). But so does the second factor, since the items with high loadings are divorce, residence in the state of less than five years, and mortgage foreclosure. The difference seems to be that the items in factor 2 also have an economic difficulty aspect, so we might name it "Family Economic Problems."

The third factor has high loadings on unemployment, welfare, strikes, and business failures, and therefore seems to be an economic events factor. The existence of two-family factors and an economic-problems factor raises the question of whether these factors should be used as the independent variables instead of the overall SSI. We explored the utility of this strategy by computing factor-weighted indexes using the SCSS program FSCORE. We then correlated each of the three-factor score indexes with eighteen of the dependent variables and found that each of the three factors tends to be correlated with dependent variables in the same direction as the overall State Stress Index. On the average, however, the factor scores are not as highly or as consistently correlated with the dependent variables as the overall State Stress Index. This is consistent with the life events theory, which holds the critical factor is not so much the content of the stressor events but the sheer number of negative events that characterize the social climate of a state. Consequently, on both empirical and theoretical grounds, little appears to be gained, either in terms of general explanatory power or consistency in prediction of various dependent variables, by using the three-factor scores instead of the overall State Stress Index.

Two Conceptual Issues

Social Change Versus Change-Inducing Stressors

It might at first seem that an index of stressor events such as the SSI is essentially the same as a measure of the rate of social change. There is some overlap. However, the focus of the SSI is on the incidence rate of events that require an adaptive response, such as marriages, births, divorces, high school and college graduations, unemployment, and so forth. We are not measuring *change* in the marriage rate, birth rate, divorce rate, high school graduation rate, and so on. Rather, we are comparing states in which the incidence rate is high relative to other states with low incidence rates, irrespective of whether this is a long-standing pattern or represents a recent change. Each event, however, is presumed to require changes in the lives of the persons involved, and that is why the event is included.

Of course, it is possible that the same event has a different meaning if it is a new phenomenon versus a long-standing pattern to which the society has worked out adaptations. The infant death rate in India and the United States illustrates the point. Indian society has well-developed institutional mechanisms for coping with the fact that a high proportion of all children born will not survive to adulthood. Thus, while the death of a child is always stressful, it is far less so in that context than in the United States.

The above discussion suggests that both social change and the incidence rate of events that require changes in life patterns are potential stressors. However, they are conceptually separate and may have different consequences. Consequently, it is important to avoid confusing one with the other. In this research, every effort will be made to focus on the incidence of "life events" that require an adaptive response, irrespective of whether these are a new or a long-standing characteristic of the state. It would also be desirable to investigate the rate of social change and correlate that with our measures of social health; we are considering doing that in future research.

Interpretation of System Level Life Events Scores

There is an important difference between a system level variable such as the SSI and the individual level life events scales. At the individual level, the events all occur to the *same* individual, and it is the cumulative buildup of demands for adaptation that results in the stressful reaction. In the case of the SSI measure, however, we do not know that the events occur in the lives of the same individuals but only that they are occurring in the same social environment. Individual-level and system-level scores then have somewhat different interpretations and implications.

One implication is that concentration of many life events in a social system should increase the statistical probability of such events occurring in combination with others for individuals living in that system. A second implication is that the accumulation of life events that require significant change and adaptation on the part of individuals can affect the social system itself and thereby the residents and the institutional structure of communities, and thus lead to a new order of changes to which residents must adapt.[2]

States as Units for the Analysis

Regions of the United States and states are used as the units of analysis in this book. Regions are used only for the purpose of reporting and comparing the main independent and dependent variables of the study. The testing of theoretical hypothesis is done using states. Among the several reasons for using states as units for the theoretical analysis are the following:[3]

1. There are large state-to-state differences in important social, economic, and health indicators. While American society may be becoming more uniform over time, very large differences continue to exist. The various chapters of this book contain tables which array the states in rank order in respect to a variety of factors. Almost every one of these rank order listings illustrates the large differences that continue to characterize the states.

An analysis of the broader set of data in the State and Regional Indicators Archive (SRIA), done in conjunction with another study (Baron and Straus, 1986), suggests that such differences are typical of current state-to-state differences. This analysis was carried out by drawing two random samples of 25 variables each from the first 2,080 variables in the SRIA. Large differences between states were found. The median ratio between the scores for the top-ranking and bottom-ranking states shows that scores for the top-ranking were 4.2 times greater than the scores for the low states for the first sample of 25 variables and 5.2 times greater for the second sample of 25 variables.

2. States are the basic unit of government and have primary or exclusive responsibility in all spheres not allocated by the Constitution to the federal government. This includes many vital functions such as education, police, family, law, and welfare. It is at the state level that many medical, legal, and social problems are addressed. They may well be the most important budgetary and political units for dealing with stress and its consequences. States are an important basis of non-governmental social organizations as well, such as professional organizations (Sharkansky, 1970).

3. States are a source of identity and pride. Despite trends toward homogenization and population mobility, identification with states continues to be widespread. The cultural characteristics of even adjacent states are frequently perceived as sharply different. Such differences are important in the social-psychological lives of individuals.

One such neighboring state comparison that has been documented is Utah versus Nevada. Age-specific mortality rates are as much as 69 percent greater in Nevada than in Utah. Yet the two states are ". . . very much alike in respect to income, schooling, urbanization, climate, and other variables thought to be the cause of variations in mortality. What then explains the difference in death rates? The answer almost surely lies in the different life-styles of the residents of the two states" (Fuchs, 1974:53). Fuchs then goes on to list such life-style factors as religion, marital instability, alcohol and tobacco consumption, and geographic mobility. In addition, Fuchs notes: "And lest the reader think that the higher rate in Nevada is attributable to the 'sinful' atmosphere of Reno and Las Vegas, we should note that infant mortality in the rest of the state is almost exactly the same as in these two cities." Although the two examples just given are dramatic, the tables in Chapters 2, 3, and 4 show that they are by no means exceptional.

4. State-level data of the type most useful for measuring stressful events, crimes, illness, and maladaptive behaviors are all more extensively and completely covered for states in comparison to other geographical units. Some of the indicators of

variables critical for this research are not available for units smaller than states and regions.

5. The usefulness of state-level data for research has been demonstrated in research by others. Research using state-level data has many precedents. Although the largest part of this work has been in political science (because the states are central to the American political system), much work has also been done in economics, sociology, and criminology.

Taking just our own discipline of sociology, a number of studies using state-level data have been published in each of the major sociological journals in the past three years. Examples of this research include the study by Hicks, Friedland, and Johnson (1978) showing that the presence in a state of headquarters of large business and labor organizations influences the extent to which a state uses its taxing and spending powers to redistribute income; the study by Jacobs and Britt (1979) showing that the greater the degree of inequality within a state, the higher the rate of violence by the police; and the study by Stack (1980), which shows that the incidence of divorce is highly associated with the suicide rate. Each of these studies avoided such common methodological errors as failing to control for confounding variables or using too many independent variables in the regression. All of this suggests that there is a well-established and continuing tradition of high-quality research using data on American states.

Some disadvantages to using states include the following:

1. State boundaries are to a certain extent artificial in that they are not isomorphic with clearly defined economic and social systems. However, they are not meaningless in that regard either. To an equal or greater extent than is the case with cities, SMSAs, counties, and regions, states have distinctive social, cultural, and political identities, as we have suggested above.

2. Another concern is that the use of average figures for states masks their considerable internal heterogeneity. The problem of internal heterogeneity, however, is one that exists whenever a single statistic is used to represent any group such as Catholics or Jews, or any city or metropolitan area and is even more severe with national "social indicators."

Compared to the entire United States, states are clearly more homogeneous. Yet this has not deterred work on compiling and using national statistics such as those reported in *Social Indicators III* (Bureau of the Census, 1980). Nor has it prevented the development of important cross-national comparative research. If researchers are willing to accept (at least for certain purposes) a single statistic to represent the entire United States and each of about seventy nations (some as heterogeneous as India), the same logic should apply to data on individual states.

Endnotes

1. Before transforming the rates to Z scores, the distributions were inspected for outliers. When an outlier (as defined below) was located, it was replaced by a less extreme value in order to prevent that one indicator from having an overwhelming influence on the score for a state. For example, the divorce rate for Nevada (16.9) is double that of the next-highest state (8.7), and is more than six standard deviations from the mean (5.33). Consequently, for purposes of computing the score of Nevada on the SSI, the divorce rate for Nevada was changed to be just higher than the rate for the next-highest state, in this case to a rate of 9.0. Two criteria were used to define outliers: (a) a value that is one or more standard deviations from the next highest value and (b) a value that is more than 2.5 standard deviations from the mean for all states. All values that met both these criteria were replaced by a value slightly higher than the value for the next-highest state. Thus, the divorce rate for Nevada was recoded to be 9.0 before transforming the divorce rates to Z scores. Tables 3–1a, b, and c, show the distribution of the states before adjusting outliers.
2. Another way of conceptualizing the difference between system-level and individual-level variables is brought into focus by consideration of the widely cited paper by Robinson (1950) on the use of ecological correlations (i.e., correlations based on group averages). Robinson suggested that group-level data are frequently used as substitutes for the individual correlations when investigators are really interested in individuals. In retrospect it is clear that at least some of the discrepancies between ecological and individual-level correlations pointed out by Robinson are the result of failure to adequately specify the model. In fact, all of Robinson's examples are bivariate (Hanushek and Jackson, 1977:84–86). More important, analysts such as Menzel (1950) argue that the "group or social system level" is actually more meaningful for analysis of social phenomena. Our research illustrates Menzel's view. Our primary focus is on the social system level.

    There are, however, several ways in which a group level or ecological correlation can arise. First, it may arise from an aggregated individual effect. That is, the concentration of stressful life events in some communities is associated with accumulation of those life events in the lives of many residents. In turn, some of those who experience accumulated life events may suffer the consequences in the form of disabilities or deviance in the way suggested by the large body of previous literature on life events at the individual level. The concentration of such individuals in certain areas results in correlations observed at the community level. Even if this is the only process underlying our findings, it is still an addition to what was known on the basis of previous individual level research because it traces the stress link from the structure of the community to the experience of the individual. This can have important implications for primary prevention of mental illness and crime.

However, as Menzel has suggested, a new level of causal relationship or correlation may occur at the group level that is not simply a reflection of grouped individual effects as described above. For example, a 10 percent rate of unemployment affects not only the one in ten persons who may be out of work but also their families and local businesses, and may have a socially and economically depressing effect on communities throughout a state. In a similar way, states experiencing rapid population growth may present adjustment problems for their new migrants who may experience a loss of supportive relationships at the very time that stressful new demands are being presented by the environment (Fuchs, 1974; Wechsler, 1961). Such growth may also exert stress on the stationary members of the receiving communities who witness a disruption of their familiar social landscape by the sudden influx of newcomers who are different from themselves in important respects (affluence, values, age, ethnicity, etc.). In addition, accumulation of changes can affect the institutional level of communities (churches, schools, government) and by this create demands for further adaptation throughout the community.

3. These issues are covered in more detail in Jaffee and Straus (n.d.) and in Straus (1985b).

Chapter 3

LIFE STRESSES IN AMERICAN STATES AND REGIONS

A widely held belief is that we live in the midst of a highly stressful society. This may or may not be true compared with other nations or compared with previous historical periods. What is true is that the United States is far from being a homogeneous place. Like other social characteristics, social stressors are unlikely to be evenly distributed throughout the society. In fact, one of the major hypotheses of this study contends that some locations within the social system are more stressful than others.

This chapter tests that hypothesis by examining the extent to which the frequency of stressful events differs across the various states and regions of the United States. We do this by examining the geographic variations in our composite measure of stressful events—the State Stress Index. In a sense this chapter could be thought of as "a geography of stress."

The description of the spatial distribution of stressors is interesting in itself and constitutes a legitimate and important inquiry in its own right. But it also sets the stage for the later chapters in this book, which investigate whether this spatial patterning of stressors is associated with differences between states in rates of crimes, maladaptive behaviors, and disease.

How the States Rank

The Overall Stress Index

Figure 3–1 arrays the fifty states according to their score on the State Stress Index.[1] The higher the score the higher the incidence

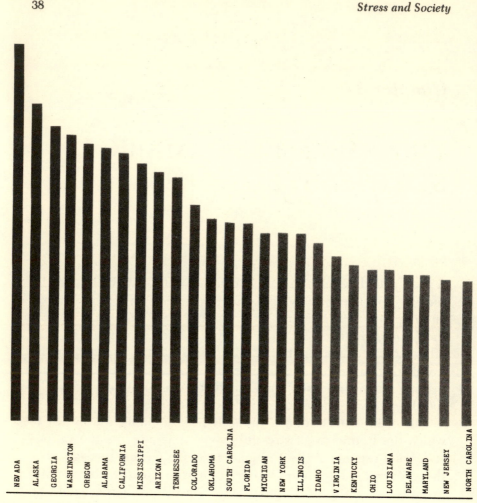

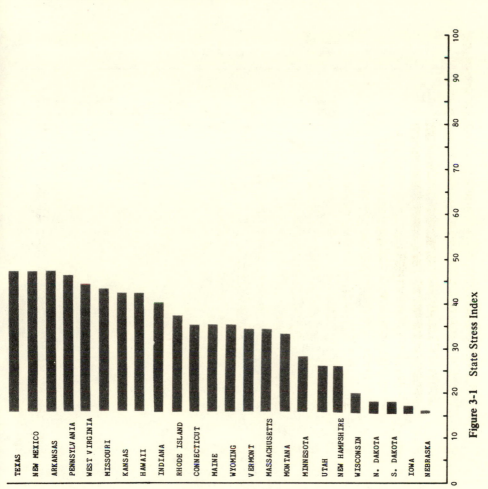

Figure 3-1   State Stress Index

Rank Order of the States for Buffer Variables

Rank	Family Integration State	ximf3	Mental Health Support State	xmhp	% Voting State	v709r	Welfare Support State	v980
1	ALAS	53	MASS	57.5	ALAS	45.02	N.Y.	371
2	UTAH	52	N.Y.	54.3	COLO	40.10	HAWA	365
3	HAWA	38	CONN	41.7	NEV	39.86	CAL	302
4	N.D.	38	MD	39.6	GA	39.79	MASS	300
5	IDA	32	CAL	35.4	MD	39.15	ALAS	296
6	S.D.	30	VT	35.3	N.H.	38.85	WISC	292
7	WYO	28	PA	31.5	VT	38.84	MICH	292
8	VT	27	COLO	29.4	S.C.	38.80	PA	283
9	N.M.	27	N.J.	28.4	N.C.	38.47	CONN	282
10	N.H.	26	MINN	28.0	WASH	38.45	N.J.	267
11	INDI	26	ILL	27.7	VA	38.44	MINN	267
12	DEL	25	R.I.	27.6	HAWA	38.33	ILL	266
13	MINN	25	OHIO	27.2	TEX	38.30	R.I.	263
14	WISC	24	N.H.	26.6	CAL	38.29	OREG	261
15	LA	21	KANS	26.4	UTAH	38.19	WASH	261
16	COLO	20	ARIZ	25.6	N.M.	38.13	VT	256
17	S.C.	20	ME	24.8	MICH	38.05	IDA	252
18	IOWA	19	HAWA	24.1	DEL	37.97	IOWA	251
19	ME	19	OREG	22.5	TENN	37.93	UTAH	247
20	MONT	19	UTAH	22.4	LA	37.84	N.D.	232
21	OHIO	18	VA	22.3	INDI	37.58	KANS	227
22	VA	18	WISC	21.7	WYO	37.22	NEBR	219
23	MICH	17	MICH	20.2	MINN	37.16	N.H.	213
24	ARIZ	17	DEL	20.1	OHIO	37.12	DEL	207
25	N.J.	16	WASH	20.1	OREG	37.08	OKLA	205
26	CONN	16	NEBR	19.9	IDA	37.04	OHIO	197
27	KY	16	ALAS	19.3	ARIZ	36.98	COLO	196
28	NEBR	16	FLA	18.0	ALA	36.87	S.D.	196
29	MD	15	TENN	17.5	ILL	36.86	WYO	195
30	MISS	15	INDI	17.0	KY	36.86	ME	194
31	GA	14	WYO	16.8	CONN	36.82	VA	190
32	TENN	14	TEX	16.6	N.Y.	36.48	W.VA	184
33	N.C.	14	KY	16.2	MONT	36.29	MONT	177
34	ALA	13	MO	15.9	WIS	36.22	MD	176
35	TEX	11	N.M.	15.8	N.J.	36.13	INDI	173
36	WASH	10	GA	15.3	MISS	36.08	KY	169
37	ARK	8	NEV	15.1	OKLA	35.98	NEV	162
38	KANS	8	LA	15.1	MASS	35.90	N.C.	154
39	OREG	7	N.C.	15.0	MO	35.54	N.M.	150
40	OKLA	6	MONT	14.7	ARK	35.53	MO	148
41	NEV	5	OKLA	14.1	ME	35.49	ARIZ	141
42	W.VA	5	ARK	13.9	W.VA	35.28	FLA	140
43	ILL	4	N.D.	13.7	NEBR	35.19	ARK	136
44	MO	2	IOWA	13.3	IOWA	35.17	LA	120
45	MASS	-1	IDA	12.6	KANS	34.84	ALA	113
46	CAL	-2	S.C.	12.2	PA	34.32	TEX	104
47	R.I.	-2	W.VA	11.6	N.D.	34.03	TENN	103
48	PA	-3	S.D.	9.0	R.I.	33.95	GA	100
49	N.Y.	-10	ALA	8.0	S.D.	32.84	S.C.	84
50	FLA	-13	MISS	7.8	FLA	31.74	MISS	47

rate of stressful events occurring in that state. Nevada has the most stressful environment of any state in the nation, with the state of Alaska in second place. Also in the highest quintile in terms of stress are the states of Georgia, Washington, Oregon, Alabama, California, Mississippi, Arizona, and Tennessee, in descending order. Although these states vary widely in terms of their social and economic characteristics, all of them are located either in the western part of the United States or in the South. Interestingly, there are no states in this group from either the old industrial North or from the agricultural heartland of the Midwest.

At the opposite end of the spectrum are the least stressful states, led by Nebraska, which has a lower incidence rate of stressful events than any state in the union. Also among the least stressful states are Iowa, South Dakota, North Dakota, Wisconsin, New Hampshire, Utah, Minnesota, Montana, Massachusetts, and Vermont, in ascending order. The ten states in the low-stress quintile are almost all located in the central plains or upper New England.

Interesting differences between individual states are evident. For example, the two newest states, Alaska and Hawaii, appear to differ sharply in terms of the total stressfulness of their environments. Alaska is second from highest, while Hawaii ranks thirty-fifth on the index of stressful events.

Nevada and Utah are two contiguous states that are often compared by social analysts in terms of their geographic similarity and cultural differences. Fuchs, for example, in an essay entitled "Tale of Two States" (1974), points out that Utah residents are among the most healthy in the United States, while Nevada is nearly at the opposite end of the spectrum, despite the similarity in climate, income levels, degree of urbanization, and availability of medical care in these two states. He attributed the disparity to differences in life-style. As indicated in Figure 3–1, Nevada appears to be the most stressful state in the country, while Utah ranks forty-fourth among all states—clearly one of the least stressful states in the country.

In a preliminary study we developed a "positive" stress index based only on life events that are generally regarded as desirable in our culture. These events included marriages, births, improvements in income, graduation from school, and so forth. When states are arranged according to their rank on this positive stress index, Utah ranks first among the fifty states, while Nevada moves to forty-seventh place. Thus, while both states may be considered stressful from the standpoint of the number of life events that require adjustment, the quality of those life events is directly antithetical between Utah and Nevada.

Individual Stressors in High and Low Stress States

The analyses to be reported in the following chapters measure the stressfulness of the environment through the State Stress Index, which combines the incidence rates for fifteen stressor events. This follows Holmes and Rahe's theoretical approach which emphasizes the cumulative effect of multiple events rather than the quality of particular kinds of events. There is a practical reason as well. It would impede both the analysis and the exposition to refer repeatedly to all fifteen separate types of events. At this point, however, examining how some of the individual events and subgroups of events are geographically distributed is helpful to understand why particular states and regions are high and low in the overall SSI. To do this, we will examine the two states with the highest scores on the SSI—Nevada and Alaska.

Nevada. On average the most stressful state in the country, Nevada was among the highest states across a broad spectrum of states experiencing stressful events. For one thing, it has been growing at a phenomenal rate. Since World War II, no other state has experienced a comparable growth rate.

Nevada has a long history of overnight booms, beginning with the gold and silver rushes of the nineteenth century. Today, it remains literally a "frontier" state, in the sense that 35 percent of its population has been living in the state less than five years. Nevada in this regard is second only to Alaska, with its 41 percent recent migrants (see Table 3–1c, column 2).

The constant influx helps to create a pattern of social instability. Recent residents have to make new friends, and this process is itself a strain. The absence of social support and social controls for conformity, which an established network of friends and relatives usually provides, is another important source of instability. Ironically, in rapidly growing communities, the "natives" tend to feel threatened and react by being cool to newcomers, making it even harder for newcomers to establish a new social network. Of course, in such rapidly growing communities, it may not only be the newcomers who are affected. Long-time residents may be affected by the sudden changes in their familiar social landscape caused by the influx.

A primary draw to the state of Nevada in recent decades has been the spectacularly successful gambling industry. Other factors attract populations to Nevada, such as a resurgent mining industry in precious metals, pro-industry tax laws, and the emergence of Nevada as a distribution and warehousing center for the West. However, it remains an essentially "one-industry state." Peirce and Hagstrom (1983) estimate that 32 percent of the population make their living directly from the gaming business and 25 percent in related businesses.

Nevada shows a long history of lack of concern with conventional morality, as exemplified not only by the casinos but also by legal prostitution and easy divorce laws. The easy divorce laws, "quickie marriage chapels," and many out-of-staters coming in for divorces undoubtedly contribute to extremely high resident divorce rates; in fact, they are the highest in the nation, even after allowing for non-residents. The operation of gaming houses on a 24-hour basis may create personal strains for employees themselves and their marriages and children.

The "fast buck" atmosphere spawned by the culture of the gaming industry may affect other areas of life as well. It may help to explain the highest-in-the-nation rate of personal bankruptcies in Nevada and a high rate of mortgage foreclosures as well (see Table 3–1a, columns 4 and 5). The instability of the state's economic institutions is further reflected in the high rates of unemployment claims (third highest in the nation) and in the high numbers of workers on strike (second highest in the nation).

Because of the pervading emphasis on the "fast buck" and "good times," the state may attract unhappy individuals, dissatisfied with their previous life, who hope to find quick success and contentment "among the glitter and lights of Las Vegas" (Peirce and Hagstrom, 1983). Such a population would be likely candidates for a variety of personal and social problems.

Alaska. The second most stressful state in the union is Alaska. Like the state of Nevada, it experienced phenomenal growth in recent years and has a history of periodic booms and busts extending back to the nineteenth century. The more spectacular of these booms included the great Yukon Gold Rush of the nineteenth century, the military buildup during and following World War II,

	ECONOMIC STRESSORS					
	Business Failures Per Million Pop.		Unemployment Initial Claims Per 100K Adults		Workers on Strike Per 100K Adults	
Rank	State	v382r	State	v452r	State	t58r
1	WASH	108.8	ALAS	34.4	W.VA	16.29
2	OREG	102.1	ME	27.2	NEV	5.35
3	N.J.	89.9	NEV	26.7	KY	4.81
4	OKLA	68.3	R.I.	25.3	ALAS	4.65
5	MD	66.6	WASH	21.6	OHIO	3.73
6	MICH	63.1	MICH	19.8	MICH	3.39
7	MINN	62.3	OREG	19.5	PA	2.95
8	MASS	62.1	PA	19.5	INDI	2.46
9	CAL	59.3	CONN	19.2	IOWA	2.42
10	ALAS	57.5	N.C.	18.7	ALA	2.38
11	N.Y.	56.6	CAL	17.0	ILL	2.00
12	N.H.	55.9	S.C.	16.5	MO	1.90
13	NEV	52.4	VT	15.9	VA	1.90
14	ARIZ	52.4	N.Y.	15.3	TENN	1.75
15	TENN	50.7	MO	15.3	WASH	1.57
16	IDA	50.5	N.J.	15.2	MASS	1.51
17	ILL	45.1	ARK	14.8	N.J.	1.37
18	GA	45.0	DEL	14.7	N.Y.	1.31
19	PA	44.0	IDA	14.2	N.M.	1.20
20	OHIO	39.6	N.H.	13.5	ARIZ	1.11
21	CONN	39.4	MASS	13.4	ME	1.10
22	VT	37.8	WIS	13.4	R.I.	1.09
23	WIS	37.5	MONT	13.2	CAL	1.03
24	N.D.	35.7	GA	12.8	WIS	1.02
25	VA	34.1	ALA	12.3	D.C.	0.99
26	TEX	33.6	ILL	12.0	CONN	0.97
27	FLA	30.8	INDI	11.9	KANS	0.96
28	NEBR	30.2	OHIO	11.7	OREG	0.93
29	D.C.	28.4	KY	11.6	IDA	0.92
30	ALA	26.7	TENN	11.3	S.D.	0.88
31	ARK	25.6	HAWA	11.1	MINN	0.87
32	MO	25.1	W.VA	10.9	WYO	0.78
33	INDI	24.7	ARIZ	10.8	DEL	0.76
34	ME	24.3	MD	10.6	MD	0.76
35	KY	23.9	D.C.	9.7	NEBR	0.67
36	MONT	23.9	UTAH	9.6	GA	0.60
37	IOWA	23.3	N.D.	9.5	MONT	0.59
38	COLO	23.2	N.M.	9.3	OKLA	0.59
39	KANS	20.7	COLO	9.3	ARK	0.54
40	S.D.	20.4	MINN	9.0	HAWA	0.53
41	UTAH	16.2	MISS	8.8	UTAH	0.53
42	LA	14.8	LA	8.5	COLO	0.46
43	N.M.	14.5	FLA	8.5	MISS	0.46
44	MISS	14.4	OKLA	7.7	TEX	0.41
45	N.C.	12.6	IOWA	7.6	N.C.	0.40
46	S.C.	11.2	VA	7.2	LA	0.37
47	W.VA	10.4	NEBR	7.1	N.H.	0.36
48	DEL	10.3	KANS	6.5	VT	0.31
49	R.I.	4.3	S.D.	5.9	FLA	0.28
50	HAWA	1.1	WYO	5.8	N.D.	0.24
51	WYO	0.0	TEX	5.3	S.C.	0.11

Table 3-1a   State Stress Index and Component Indicators.

	ECON. (cont.)				FAMILY STRESSORS			
	Personal Bankruptcies Per 100K Pop.		Mortgage Foreclosures Per 100K Pop.		Divorces Per 1,000 Pop.		Abortions Per 100K Pop.	
Rank	State	t183r	State	t200r	State	t57	State	z120r1
1	NEV	312	ARIZ	7619	NEV	16.9	D.C.	4565
2	ALA	214	GA	5412	ARK	8.7	N.Y.	1040
3	TENN	204	MISS	4715	ALAS	8.4	CAL	996
4	KANS	202	S.C.	4701	ARIZ	8.4	HAWA	942
5	CAL	189	NEV	4445	N.M.	7.8	WASH	893
6	INDI	189	COLO	3997	OKLA	7.8	ALAS	762
7	IDA	182	MICH	3385	FLA	7.5	COLO	736
8	COLO	181	OKLA	3295	WASH	7.5	TENN	727
9	ARIZ	176	CAL	2866	WYO	7.3	NEV	717
10	KY	174	TEX	2710	IDA	6.9	MASS	683
11	GA	173	FLA	2710	OREG	6.9	FLA	674
12	OREG	173	DEL	2605	COLO	6.8	KANS	659
13	VA	156	ILL	2389	ALA	6.6	GA	659
14	ILL	155	LA	2370	TENN	6.4	OREG	657
15	OKLA	151	INDI	2122	MONT	6.4	ILL	652
16	ME	149	WASH	2014	TEX	6.4	N.J.	619
17	OHIO	144	OHIO	1985	GA	6.3	MICH	589
18	LA	138	N.J.	1965	CAL	6.2	MD	584
19	NEBR	134	ALA	1769	INDI	5.9	TEX	574
20	MO	133	MINN	1739	DEL	5.6	VA	570
21	WASH	130	MO	1674	KANS	5.6	OHIO	566
22	WYO	129	VT	1634	OHIO	5.5	N.M.	544
23	N.M.	128	N.C.	1569	HAWA	5.3	CONN	544
24	MISS	124	TENN	1310	MO	5.3	PA	531
25	MONT	115	MASS	1299	N.H.	5.3	DEL	526
26	W.VA	111	HAWA	1250	ME	5.2	VT	505
27	IOWA	108	PA	1240	MISS	5.2	N.C.	463
28	MINN	103	CONN	1229	UTAH	5.0	R.I.	460
29	WIS	100	VA	1157	W.VA	4.9	MINN	440
30	UTAH	100	N.H.	1071	MICH	4.7	N.H.	422
31	MICH	90	ARK	1067	KY	4.7	ARIZ	422
32	VT	82	N.Y.	928	ILL	4.6	LA	389
33	N.C.	81	OREG	910	D.C.	4.4	OKLA	373
34	ARK	80	MD	867	N.C.	4.4	NEBR	354
35	N.Y.	80	KY	856	VA	4.2	WIS	353
36	CONN	79	D.C.	785	VT	4.0	KY	339
37	N.H.	71	IOWA	697	MD	3.9	ALA	325
38	FLA	70	ALAS	662	CONN	3.8	S.C.	318
39	R.I.	69	UTAH	651	NEBR	3.8	MO	315
40	ALAS	67	WIS	580	IOWA	3.8	ME	313
41	N.D.	65	N.M.	530	S.C.	3.7	N.D.	305
42	HAWA	61	NEBR	528	MINN	3.5	MONT	305
43	MASS	61	KANS	458	R.I.	3.5	UTAH	251
44	S.D.	58	IDA	410	S.D.	3.4	IOWA	247
45	DEL	56	ME	404	LA	3.3	WYO	242
46	N.J.	54	WYO	207	WIS	3.2	IDA	210
47	PA	50	W.VA	203	PA	3.1	S.D.	208
48	TEX	38	R.I.	157	N.Y.	3.0	INDI	197
49	MD	37	MONT	131	N.J.	3.0	ARK	168
50	D.C.	34	S.D.	28	N.D.	2.9	W.VA	124
51	S.C.	20	N.D.	15	MASS	2.9	MISS	119

Table 3-1b   State Stress Index and Component Indicators (Continued).

| | FAMILY STRESSOR (Continued) | | | | | | OTHER STRESSORS | |
| | Illegitimate Births Per 1,000 Pop. | | Infant Deaths Per 1K Births | | Fetal Deaths Per 1K Births | | Disaster Assistance Per 100K Pop. | |
Rank	State	t207rm	State	t70r	State	t64r	State	t187r2
1	D.C.	8.7	D.C.	24.5	D.C.	26.5	IDA	307.0
2	MISS	5.9	MISS	21.4	MISS	16.2	TENN	95.3
3	LA	5.3	ALA	19.7	GA	14.2	ALA	90.0
4	S.C.	4.4	S.C.	19.4	S.C.	14.0	OKLA	67.7
5	GA	4.3	LA	17.7	VA	13.6	N.Y.	64.3
6	ALA	4.0	N.C.	17.7	R.I.	13.4	N.J.	60.4
7	ILL	3.9	WYO	17.4	HAWA	13.4	PA	59.3
8	DEL	3.7	MD	17.1	TENN	12.5	N.D.	47.3
9	MD	3.5	ILL	16.7	COLO	12.4	D.C.	47.1
10	ARK	3.5	W.VA	16.6	N.C.	12.4	MISS	46.0
11	ALAS	3.3	S.D.	16.5	ALA	12.1	W.VA	43.0
12	ARIZ	3.2	OKLA	16.5	PA	12.1	CONN	42.2
13	TENN	3.1	VA	16.2	DEL	11.6	MASS	38.8
14	N.C.	3.1	ALAS	16.1	N.Y.	11.3	WASH	30.7
15	FLA	3.1	TENN	16.0	KY	11.2	MINN	29.9
16	N.Y.	2.9	TEX	16.0	LA	11.0	ILL	29.1
17	TEX	2.9	MONT	16.0	FLA	10.8	TEX	28.5
18	MO	2.9	N.Y.	15.9	W.VA	10.8	VA	27.2
19	MICH	2.8	GA	15.9	ILL	10.7	MICH	26.2
20	VA	2.8	ARK	15.5	TEX	10.6	MD	25.0
21	OHIO	2.7	N.M.	15.5	ARK	10.6	FLA	24.7
22	N.J.	2.6	PA	15.4	MO	10.3	MO	22.7
23	S.D.	2.6	ARIZ	15.3	N.D.	10.0	NEV	22.4
24	KY	2.5	MO	15.2	KANS	10.0	OHIO	22.4
25	CAL	2.5	MICH	15.2	WYO	9.7	INDI	21.0
26	INDI	2.5	FLA	15.0	INDI	9.6	VT	20.9
27	OKLA	2.4	OHIO	14.9	MICH	9.6	OREG	20.7
28	HAWA	2.4	N.J.	14.9	N.J.	9.6	KANS	19.8
29	NEV	2.4	KY	14.8	OKLA	9.3	ARK	18.5
30	PA	2.3	INDI	14.5	CAL	9.1	DEL	18.4
31	CONN	2.1	WASH	14.5	S.D.	9.0	LA	18.0
32	N.M.	2.1	KANS	14.2	MASS	9.0	KY	16.9
33	OREG	2.1	R.I.	14.1	OREG	8.9	ME	16.4
34	COLO	2.1	IOWA	14.1	OHIO	8.9	GA	15.1
35	W.VA	2.0	NEBR	14.1	N.M.	8.8	HAWA	14.7
36	IDA	2.0	CONN	14.0	MINN	8.7	R.I.	14.1
37	WASH	2.0	MINN	13.8	ARIZ	8.6	N.H.	13.9
38	WIS	2.0	NEV	13.7	MD	8.4	S.C.	13.5
39	KANS	2.0	N.D.	13.4	WIS	8.3	IOWA	13.0
40	MONT	2.0	IDA	13.3	WASH	8.3	MONT	12.7
41	MASS	1.9	DEL	13.0	CONN	8.3	WIS	11.0
42	R.I.	1.8	COLO	12.9	IOWA	8.2	UTAH	10.4
43	ME	1.8	OREG	12.6	UTAH	8.1	S.D.	9.6
44	NEBR	1.8	WIS	12.5	MONT	8.0	CAL	9.3
45	N.D.	1.8	CAL	12.4	NEBR	8.0	NEBR	7.5
46	WYO	1.8	VT	12.1	NEV	8.0	ARIZ	7.4
47	MINN	1.8	MASS	12.1	ALAS	7.3	ALAS	6.3
48	VT	1.7	UTAH	11.8	IDA	7.0	N.M.	6.3
49	IOWA	1.5	N.H.	11.7	N.H.	6.9	N.C.	6.2
50	N.H.	1.4	HAWA	11.0	VT	6.1	COLO	4.4
51	UTAH	1.3	ME	11.0	ME	5.4	WYO	1.8

Table 3-1c   State Stress Index and Component Indicators (Continued).

			OTHER STRESSORS (Continued)					
	State Resident Less than 5 yrs: % of Adult Pop.		New Houses Authorized Per 1,000 Pop.		New Welfare Cases Per 100K Pop.		High School Dropouts Per 100K Pop.	
Rank	State	p16ß	State	v536r	State	t191r2	State	t182r
1	ALAS	41.0	NEV	22.13	CAL	1858	D.C.	1047
2	NEV	35.3	UTAH	14.90	OREG	1665	MISS	979
3	ARIZ	32.5	WASH	13.01	VT	1533	N.C.	903
4	FLA	26.3	WYO	12.05	COLO	1435	S.C.	895
5	COLO	25.1	OREG	11.55	WASH	1325	GA	870
6	WYO	23.0	ARIZ	11.06	KY	1261	LA	773
7	IDA	20.9	ALAS	10.99	W.VA	1227	ALAS	741
8	HAWA	20.8	CAL	10.25	OHIO	1172	KY	728
9	N.M.	20.4	IDA	10.23	N.Y.	1136	ALA	692
10	OREG	19.0	HAWA	9.47	ME	1134	TEX	680
11	D.C.	18.8	COLO	9.45	KANS	1129	DEL	669
12	N.H.	18.8	N.D.	9.02	PA	1113	N.Y.	649
13	VA	17.9	FLA	7.86	DEL	1109	W.VA	624
14	UTAH	17.6	TEX	7.83	NEV	1096	FLA	621
15	WASH	16.5	VA	7.81	R.I.	1093	VA	621
16	DEL	16.4	N.M.	7.36	MD	1088	N.M.	611
17	MONT	15.2	WIS	7.03	UTAH	1077	MD	590
18	MD	15.1	IOWA	6.86	MICH	1061	ME	584
19	VT	15.0	S.D.	6.85	D.C.	983	R.I.	568
20	ARK	14.8	KANS	6.71	GA	981	ILL	561
21	OKLA	14.4	N.H.	6.57	MASS	980	ARK	555
22	TEX	14.4	MD	6.42	S.C.	972	MICH	550
23	CAL	13.6	MINN	6.25	MONT	968	INDI	530
24	ME	13.1	MONT	6.24	IDA	961	OHIO	514
25	NEBR	13.0	NEBR	6.12	N.M.	957	OKLA	499
26	GA	12.7	S.C.	5.65	WIS	954	MO	477
27	N.D.	12.4	OKLA	5.31	HAWA	939	CONN	476
28	KANS	12.4	ILL	5.31	ARK	936	TENN	469
29	TENN	11.4	INDI	5.28	MO	909	MASS	465
30	ALA	11.1	R.I.	4.96	LA	895	OREG	464
31	CONN	11.0	MICH	4.93	MISS	883	CAL	463
32	S.C.	10.9	ALA	4.80	TENN	876	N.J.	447
33	MISS	10.6	N.C.	4.75	S.D.	871	N.H.	437
34	N.J.	10.4	MO	4.69	ALAS	868	PA	429
35	S.D.	10.1	OHIO	4.60	FLA	861	VT	427
36	LA	10.1	GA	4.51	MINN	859	IDA	414
37	R.I.	9.9	DEL	4.47	ILL	836	HAWA	398
38	MO	9.4	TENN	4.41	N.J.	832	S.D.	385
39	W.VA	9.3	LA	4.35	OKLA	831	WYO	381
40	N.C.	9.2	CONN	4.27	IOWA	816	KANS	376
41	MASS	9.2	N.J.	4.17	ALA	815	MONT	370
42	MINN	9.2	ARK	3.84	N.C.	764	N.D.	344
43	IOWA	8.7	PA	3.63	WYO	717	NEV	339
44	KY	8.7	KY	3.56	VA	699	COLO	327
45	INDI	8.6	ME	3.55	CONN	698	WASH	318
46	ILL	7.6	MASS	3.43	INDI	686	NEBR	313
47	WIS	7.5	VT	3.36	ARIZ	678	IOWA	313
48	PA	6.0	D.C.	3.13	N.H.	665	ARIZ	306
49	N.Y.	5.9	MISS	2.76	TEX	620	UTAH	299
50	OHIO	5.8	N.Y.	1.62	NEBR	586	WIS	284
51	MICH	5.5	W.VA	0.93	N.D.	530	MINN	254

Table 3-1d   State Stress Index and Component Indicators (Continued).

and more recently, the North Slope Oil Strike and the construction of the Alaskan Pipe Line.

The state grew an astounding 33 percent during the decade from 1970 to 1980. It had more new residents (41 percent living in their present residence less than five years) than any state in the union and thus could be expected to experience all of the personal and community strains inherent in such growth.

Peirce and Hagstrom (1983) suggest that never in the history of America has a single bonanza enriched a state as did oil in Alaska. Ironically, despite the immense wealth from the oil and gas bonanza, the state was also highest in the rate of unemployment claims. News of the pipeline drew hordes of workers from other states, many of whom could not be absorbed into the work force. Recently, the state has tried to discourage poorly planned migration to the state. The turbulence of the economic system is also reflected in Table 3–1a by a relatively high rate of business failures and the rate of workers on strike—important components of the stress index.

The state retains elements of its raucous frontier past, and men heavily outnumber women. Under such conditions, it is difficult for family life to flourish. Consistent with this, Alaska is among the highest states in terms of the rates of divorce, abortions, and illegitimacy (see Table 3–1b).

Alaska's su stantial native population of Eskimos, Aleuts, and Indians have been subject to extreme stress. Many have been forced within the short space of a few decades to make the transition from a subsistence type hunting and fishing economy to a modern technological and capitalistic society. Some have been unexpectedly enriched through the Alaskan Native Claims Settlement Act of 1971, which made millions of dollars available to hastily formed native corporations that engage in basic industries such as fishing, canning, timber, and mineral excavations. However, the unemployment rate of native Americans is still exceptionally high, as is the rate of family breakups.

The extreme climate of Alaska, with its long frigid winters, may be a further source of stress, although climate appears unrelated to the type of stress reflected in our State Stress Index. Many Alaskans are confined indoors during the long, dark, and bitterly cold winters and may experience "cabin fever" from the resulting monotony. Thus Alaskans may suffer stress from both extremes: from too many changes as reflected in our State Stress Index and from the stifling monotony of forced inactivity from being shut in during the winter months.

Low Stress States.   At the opposite end of the continuum is the state of Nebraska (lowest stress), followed very closely by Iowa, South Dakota, and North Dakota. All are "cornbelt" states that share a number of common characteristics, including their dependence on either agriculture or industry related to agriculture. These states offer the advantage of small town and rural life. Even with the development of other industry in recent years, the states have managed to retain a rural atmosphere. For the most part, these states are politically and socially conservative.

Nebraska, the least stressful state on average, ranked forty-seventh in unemployment claims, forty-second in mortgage fore-closures, thirty-ninth in divorces, forty-fourth in both illegitimate births and in fetal deaths. The state ranked low on the number of families assisted for disasters (fortieth), forty-sixth on new welfare cases, and forty-sixth in the number of high school drop-outs. In fact, the state did not rank highly on any of the fifteen indicators of stressful life events. Thus comparatively few stressful life events from any source, either economic or familial, disturbed the tranquility of Nebraska residents.

Other States.   So far we have mentioned only those few states that occupy the extreme positions in regard to the stressfulness of their environments, in what is in fact a continuum. While space does not allow a discussion of the specific stressors for each of the fifty states, this information is given in Table 3–1 so that readers who are interested in a specific state can examine its profile on the several indicators that make up the State Stress Index. Since some readers will also be interested in the District of Columbia, it is included in the state rankings of individual stressors, even though D.C. was excluded when computing the SSI.

Regional Differences in Life Stressors

Regional Patterns in the Overall SSI

Figures 3–2a and 3–2b present a somewhat different way of looking at the geographic patterns of stressful events. Each division or region is composed of usually contiguous states which presumably have both a spatial and sociocultural identity. Figure 3–2a shows the mean SSI scores for the nine census divisions of the United

50   *Stress and Society*

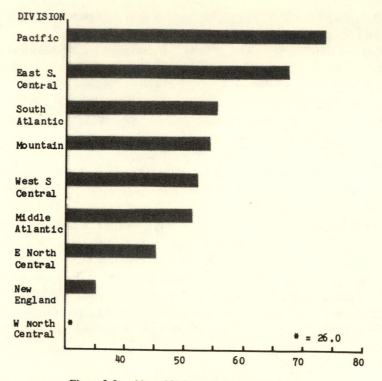

Figure 3-2a   Mean SSI Score by Census Divisions

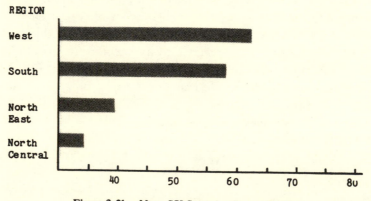

Figure 3-2b   Mean SSI Score by Census Region

States, and Figure 3–2b compares the four census regions of the United States.

Census Divisions. The Pacific division, which includes the states of Alaska, Hawaii, Washington, Oregon, and California, has the highest average stress level of any of the nine divisions of the country.

Although stress levels for the Pacific states are on average higher than for any other division, there is important variation within the division. Hawaii, as mentioned earlier, ranks only thirty-fourth in the State Stress Index and thus would have to be considered a relatively unstressful place to live. The other states in the region—Alaska, Washington, Oregon, and California—all rank within the highest quintile in terms of stressfulness of their social environment.

Pacific states are among the last settled in the country and include the states most recently admitted to the Union; in the last few decades they have experienced an unusually rapid rate of growth. In a sense, they share a kind of frontier psychology.

The Pacific states also have a history of turbulent and unsteady growth, characterized from the beginning by periodic booms and busts or cutbacks that have brought social disorganization in their wake. For example, California and Alaska experienced early gold rushes. The state of Washington experienced several periods of lurching growth following abrupt changes in the fortunes of the lumbering and airplane industries. And Alaska has continued the pattern of growth and recession now tied to the fortunes of gas and oil. Other divisions in descending order of mean stressfulness are the East South Central, the South Atlantic, and the Mountain regions.

Some divisions are clearly much less stressful than others. The least stressful census division on average is the West North Central, which includes the states of Minnesota, Wisconsin, North and South Dakota, and Nebraska. The second-least stressful division is New England. Within the New England area, there are also important subregional differences. New Hampshire (forty-fifth in the country), followed in order of increasing SSI scores by Massachusetts (forty-first), Vermont (fortieth), and Maine (thirty-eighth). Connecticut (thirty-seventh) and Rhode Island (thirty-sixth) are highest among the New England states, although not high by national comparisons. The upper New England area where low stressfulness prevails is not strictly rural but is still characterized primarily by small town life.

Census Regions. In Figure 3–2b, the nine divisions are grouped into four major regions. When the United States is divided into the four major regions, it is the West and South that stand out as the most stressful, and the North Central and the Northeast that have the least stressful social environments.

Regional Patterns of Specific Stressors

In Table 3–2, the first row of data for each stressor event enables the different regions to be compared, and the second row of data for each stressor event enables the nine census divisions to be compared with each other. There are large differences between regions and divisions for all fifteen stressful events, and most of these differences are statistically significant.

- *West North Central* states (see "WNC" under "N. Central") were low in almost all categories of events.
- *Pacific* states (see "PA" under "West") were especially high in terms of business failures, unemployment claims, divorces, abortions, new residents, new houses, and new welfare recipients.
- *Mountain* states were high on bankruptcies, divorces, infant mortality, fetal deaths, families receiving disaster assistance, new residents, and new houses.
- *South Atlantic* states were high on mortgages foreclosed, infant and fetal deaths, and students dropping out of high school.
- *Mid-Atlantic* states were high in business failures, abortions, new welfare cases, and high school drop-outs.
- *New England* states were high only in unemployment claims.
- *East North Central* states were high only with regard to strikes.
- *West South Central* states, on the other hand, were high mainly in the area of mortgage foreclosures.

Some Social-Structural Correlates of Stress

Control Variables

In addition to hypothesizing large differences in stress between geograpahic units, we also assumed that stress is unequally distributed among subgroups within geographic units. If this were a study of individual persons, this assumption could be tested by comparing people occupying different positions in the social structure—for example, rich and poor; males and females; and whites, blacks, and other races. The same principles also apply to social systems. They vary in wealth, sex ratio, racial composition, and in many other ways. The question to be addressed is whether these variations in structural characteristics are also related to the stressfulness of the society.

The extent to which social-structural factors are associated with stress needs to be determined because of the intrinsic importance of that information. Such an association also has implications for understanding the links between stress and crime, violence, and illness. The methodological point is that these variables might produce "spurious correlations" between the SSI and the dependent variables. This could occur if the social-structural variables are related to both the level of stress and the rate of crime, violence, and illness. For example, if the urbanism of the state is correlated with both stress and crime, a correlation between stress and crime might reflect the effects of urbanism rather than a distinct stress-crime relationship. Our choice of social-structural factors therefore focused on variables that are plausibly correlated with both stress and the dependent variables.

With an *N* of fifty states, there are limitations on the number of independent variables that can be included in a regression analysis. This required selecting a small number of social-structural control variables. We thought that this would mean some difficult choices because we expected to find high correlations of stress with a sizable number of variables that are also associated with crime, violence, and illness. That, however, did not turn out to be the case, as will be seen from the correlations to be presented below for each of the four social-structural variables selected for inclusion in the research.

Percent Metro. Percent Metro is the percentage of the population of the state living in "Standard Metropolitan Statistical Areas" (SMSAs) in 1970. We found a correlation of .32 between Percent Metro and the SSI, indicating that the more urban the state, the higher the stress. This is a substantial and statistically significant correlation. It confirms the widely held belief that urban life is more stressful than rural life and also indicates the importance of controlling for the Percent Metro when investigating the relationship between stress and other variables.

Percent Age 15–24 and Percent Age 55 and Over. These are

Mean For Each Census Region (1st Row) and Division (2nd Row)

Stressor Event	N.East (region)	NE	MA	N.Central (region)	ENC	WNC	South (region)	SA	ESC	WSC	West (region)	MT	PA	ANOVA F*
State Stress Index	39.4	33.5	51.3	34.3	45.8	26.0	58.2	56.3	68.5	51.8	61.7	54.9	72.6	8.16** / 5.52**
A. Economic Stressors														
Business Failures per million pop. (v382r)	46.1	37.3	63.6	35.7	42.0	31.1	29.9	27.8	29.0	35.6	43.3	29.2	65.8	1.23 / 2.03
Unemployment Init. Claims per 100K adults (v452r)	18.3	19.1	16.7	10.7	13.8	8.8	11.2	12.2	11.0	9.1	15.6	12.4	20.8	5.01** / 3.85**
Workers on Strike per 100K adults (t58r)	1.2	0.9	1.9	1.7	2.5	1.1	2.0	2.5	2.4	0.5	1.5	1.4	1.7	0.20 / 0.45
Personal Bankruptcies per 100,000 pop. (t183r)	77.5	85.5	61.4	123.9	136.1	115.1	109.9	82.4	179.3	102.2	150.0	165.9	124.5	3.25* / 3.07**
Mortgage foreclosures per 100,000 pop. (t200r)	1103.5	966.2	1378.3	1300.5	2092.6	734.7	2241.8	223.8	2163.3	2361.1	1976.8	2249.3	1540.9	1.53 / 0.92

* = $p < .05$; ** = $p < .01$ with 1 and 8 df.

NE = New England: CN, MA, NH, VT, ME; MA = Middle Atlantic: NY, NJ, PA; ENC = East North Central: OH, IN, IL, MI, WI; WNC = West North Central: MN, IA, MO, ND, SD, NE, KS; SA = South Atlantic: DE, MD, DC, VA, WV, NC, SC, GA, FL; ESC = East South Central: KY, TN, AL, MS; WSC = West South Central: AR, LA, OK, TX; MT = Mountain: MT, ID, WY, CO, NM, AZ, UT, NV; PA = Pacific: WA, OR, CA, AK, HI.

Table 3-2   Stressful Life Events by Census Region and Division.

Mean For Each Census Region (1st Row) and Division (2nd Row)

Stressor Event	N.East (mean)	NE	MA	N.Central (mean)	ENC	WNC	South (mean)	SA	ESC	WSC	West (mean)	MT	PA	ANOVA F*
State Stress Index	39.4	33.5	51.3	34.3	45.8	26.0	58.2	56.3	68.5	51.8	61.7	54.9	72.6	8.16** / 5.52**
B. Family Stressors														
Divorces per thousand pop. (t57)	3.8	4.1	3.0	4.4	4.8	4.0	5.5	5.0	5.7	6.6	7.7	8.2	6.9	10.10** / 4.35**
Abortions per 100,000 pop. (z120r1)	569.0	488.1	730.8	407.5	471.6	361.7	676.8	943.1	377.8	376.6	590.9	428.6	850.6	0.44 / 0.83
Illegitimate births per 1K pop. (t207rm)	2.0	1.7	2.5	2.4	2.8	2.1	3.9	4.0	3.9	3.6	2.3	2.1	2.5	5.52** / 2.11
Infant Deaths per 1K births (t70r)	13.5	12.5	15.5	14.6	14.8	14.5	17.3	17.3	18.0	16.5	14.1	14.5	13.4	9.07** / 4.24**
Fetal Deaths per 1K births (t64r)	9.1	8.2	11.0	9.3	9.5	9.2	12.7	13.6	13.0	10.4	9.1	8.9	9.5	6.05** / 3.05**
Disaster Assistance per 100K pop. (t187r2)	36.7	24.4	61.4	21.7	22.0	24.5	35.4	21.7	62.1	33.2	35.0	46.6	16.4	0.29 / 0.68

* = p <.05; ** = p <.01 with 1 and 8 df.

NE = New England: CN, MA, NH, VT, ME; MA = Middle Atlantic: NY, NJ, PA; ENC = East North Central: OH, IN, IL, MI, WI
WNC = West North Central: MN, IA, MO, ND, SD, NE, KS; SA = South Atlantic: DE, MD, DC, VA, WV, NC, SC, GA, FL; ESC = East
South Central: KY, TN, AL, MS; WSC = West South Central: AR, LA, OK, TX; MT = Mountain: MT, ID, WY, CO, NM, AZ, UT, NV; PA =
Pacific: WA, OR, CA, AK, HI.

Table 3-2   Stressful Life Events by Census Region and Division (Continued).

Mean For Each Census Region (1st Row) and Division (2nd Row)

Stressor Event	N.East		N.Central		South			West		ANOVA F*
	NE	MA	ENC	WNC	SA	ESC	WSC	MT	PA	
State Stress Index (region mean)	39.4		34.3			58.2		61.7		8.16**
(divisions)	33.5	51.3	45.8	26.0	56.3	68.5	51.8	54.9	72.6	5.52**
C. Other Stressors										
State Resident < than 5 yrs: % of adult pop. (p168) (region mean)	11.0		9.2			13.7		23.1		16.63**
(divisions)	12.8	7.4	7.0	10.7	15.2	10.5	13.4	23.8	22.2	7.12**
New Houses authorized per 1,000 pop. (v536r) (region mean)	4.0		6.1			4.9		11.4		24.29**
(divisions)	4.4	3.1	5.4	6.6	5.1	3.9	5.3	11.7	11.1	8.84**
New Welfare Cases per 100,000 pop. (t191r2) (region mean)	1021.0		867.8			930.0		1119.3		2.41
(divisions)	1017.8	1027.3	942.1	814.8	965.4	959.1	821.1	986.6	1331.6	1.95
High School dropouts per 100,000 pop. (t182r) (region mean)	498.4		409.1			719.0		418.3		17.69**
(divisions)	493.3	508.6	488.4	352.4	760.6	717.3	627.1	381.5	477.3	8.00**

* = p <.05; ** = p <.01 with 1 and 8 df.

NE = New England: CN, MA, NH, VT, ME; MA = Middle Atlantic: NY, NJ, PA; ENC = East North Central: OH, IN, IL, MI, WI WNC = West North Central: MN, IA, MO, ND, SD, NE, KS; SA = South Atlantic: DE, MD, DC, VA, WV, NC, SC, GA, FL; ESC = East South Central: KY, TN, AL, MS; WSC = West South Central: AR, LA, OK, TX; MT = Mountain: MT, ID, WY, CO, NM, AZ, UT, NV; PA = Pacific: WA, OR, CA, AK, HI.

Table 3-2   Stressful Life Events by Census Region and Division (Continued).

the percentages of the population of each state who were 15 through 24 years old, and those age 55 and over in 1976. The 15–24 age group was included in the study because some of the prior research shows that young people experience more stressful events (Holmes and Masuda, 1974) and are also most heavily involved in crime.

Contrary to our expectations, we found a slight negative correlation ($-.12$), which is not statistically significant—that is, a slight tendency for the proportion of people in the 15–24 age group to be associated with *low* stress.

The 55 and over age group was included because of the need to control for the fact that states with a large elderly population will have high rates for illnesses such as heart disease and cancer. However, although the percentage of persons age 55 and over is significantly related to the SSI, this correlation is also negative ($-.30$). Nevertheless, to be on the safe side, we used both age variables as controls.

When Percent 15–24 and Percent 55 and Over were used as controls, they were used only one at a time. That is, Percent 15–24 was used as a statistical control in the case of crimes that are known to be especially high for younger populations, and Percent 55 and Over was used exclusively with diseases.[2]

Percent Black.   Percent Black is the percentage of the population of each state who were black in 1976. Since these data are from the Survey of Income and Education rather than a complete census count, the Census Bureau does not consider figures of less than 1 percent reliable, and therefore does not give the Percent Black for twelve states. For purposes of this study, those twelve states were coded as 0 percent black.

The correlation of the Percent Black with the stress index is .40 ($p < .01$). This substantial correlation indicates the need to control for the Percent Black when testing hypotheses about the link of stress with crime, violence, and illness. The strong relationship between the percentage of the state population that is black and the stressfulness of life also tells us something about the circumstances under which a disproportionately large number of blacks live in this country.

Percent Below Poverty.   This is the percentage of persons in each state with incomes less than the federally defined poverty levels. We expected to find a substantial correlation between poverty and the SSI because we think that poor people experience more stressful events than those who are not in such a precarious economic position. Indeed, the SSI contains several items that are at least partly indicators of poverty, such as losing a job and going on welfare. However, the correlation of the Percent Below Poverty with the stressfulness of life in each state turned out to be only .26 ($p < .06$). Evidently, the inclusion of these items in the SSI was not sufficient to confound the SSI with income level.

Part of the reason why items such as unemployment and welfare do not produce a confounding with poverty is that these two items are not as closely tied to poverty as it might seem at first. This is because the unemployment figures are not prevalence rates but the incidence of first claims for unemployment in 1976. Consequently, to be included, a person had to be employed that year. By contrast, people living in poverty, because of continued unemployment, would not be counted, since they would not be considered as a member of the labor force. Similarly, the welfare item in the SSI is not the prevalence of welfare—which would primarily be a poverty indicator—but the incidence of new claims for welfare assistance on the part of people who were not at the time receiving such assistance. In fact, these variables were selected for the stress index because they represented new demands for adjustment on the part of individuals rather than representing ongoing conditions such as poverty and chronic unemployment.

Since one of our initial concerns about the SSI was that it might be so highly correlated with variables such as Percent Below Poverty that it would lack "discriminant validity" (Campbell and Fiske, 1959), this low correlation is a welcome finding. It can also be taken as suggesting that there is no need to control for the Percent Below Poverty when regressing crime, violence, or illness variables on stress. Despite that, we decided to keep it as a control variable because so many of the dependent variables are associated with poverty.

Buffer Variables

Five other social-structural variables were examined to determine if they are related to life stresses as measured by the SSI. The choice of these five variables was based on the idea that certain social conditions can "buffer" or mitigate the effects of stress. For example, several studies have found that individuals who have strong social support are less likely to be affected by stress than more isolated individuals (Cobb, 1976; Gore, 1978, 1981; Lin et al., 1979; Hotaling, Atwell, and Linsky, 1978). The buffer theory does *not* suggest that such variables are correlated with stress. In fact, almost the opposite is necessary. However, the correlations are presented below because they are interesting in their own right and because these correlations can affect the way the buffer variables operate in the regression models presented in Chapters 5 and 6. In each case, two correlations will be mentioned. The first is for the buffer variables in their original continuous variable form, and the second is for the version of these variables, which has been dichotomized for purposes of constructing interaction terms used in Chapters 4 and 5 to test the buffer theory. We have included indicators of several of these types of buffers in this study.

Family Integration. We computed a "Family Integration Index," which is intended to reflect the extent to which the population is living with close relatives in common households as opposed to living alone or in personally isolating circumstances. This provides at least an approximate measure of the accessibility of other people who can or do provide support, esteem, intimacy, and so forth on a day-to-day basis. The protective aspects of such integration have been recognized at least since Durkheim's classic study of suicide (1897 [1951]).

The index was computed by first transforming the three component items to Z scores and then combining them as follows:

$XINF3$ = (% of families with both husband and wife present) + (% of families with own children under 18 living at home) − (% of persons living alone in their own household)

The employment of the Family Integration Index as a buffer in this study points to a paradox about the family (Straus and Hotaling, 1980: Chapter 1). The family is widely regarded as a haven from stress in both popular thinking and in the social stress and sociological literature. It is regarded as a place where one can find respite from the tensions of the world, a group that meets basic primary needs for love, esteem, and recognition. This is the basic rationale for viewing it as a buffering variable against stress in this study, and there is a long tradition in sociology for considering it so. At the same time, the family has been recognized among some schools of psychologists as a potentially conflicted and hostile group and thereby a source of psycho-pathology (Wynne, Day, and

Hisch, 1958; Bateson, Jackson, and Weakland, 1963; Mishler and Waxler, 1965). More recently, it has been recognized as one of the most stressful and violent institutions in our society by sociologists and others (Straus and Hotaling, 1980; Straus, Gelles, and Steinmetz 1980; Farrington, 1980a).

The State Stress Index itself also reflects some of the stressful events that occur within families, including divorce, abortion, miscarriages, and infant deaths. Other sources of stress within families, such as interpersonal conflicts and unsatisfactory relationships, could not be measured with available public data. Despite this we found a negative correlation between family integration and the SSI of $-.27$ ($p < .05$).

High School Education. This is the percentage of the population age 18 and over who completed four years of high school or more in 1976. It is an indicator of "human capital," which should facilitate the process of coping with stressful events if one assumes that on the average a population with more education will have more knowledge of its options and better ability to utilize community resources for dealing with problems, and in a general sense more problem-solving ability.

The correlation of $-.28$ between the percentage of the population who have completed high school and the State Stress Index has an ironic implication. It suggests that states with high scores on the SSI tend to have populations with fewer educated persons and thereby less capacity on average to cope with that stress.

The first two buffers discussed above are based on characteristics of individuals or their immediate social surroundings that can be drawn on in times of stress. The total availability of such resources—individual and family—within a community should affect the ability of communities to come to terms with stress.

The next three buffers are more clearly characteristics of the institutional structure of the communities themselves rather than aggregations of individual characteristics. As such they speak to the types of institutional protections and resources that communities make available to their members. Thus being able to cope successfully with stress may also depend on the type of community one lives in and on the type of resources available in that community.

Index of Mental Health Professional Support. This variable is composed of the number of psychiatrists, clinical psychologists, and psychiatric social workers living in the community, per 100,000 population. It is intended to reflect the availability of professional helping networks. It includes both the private practitioners as well as community mental health agencies, clinics, and institutions. In a sense such resources exist for the purpose of helping the casualties of a stressful society. This variable has a correlation of $-.10$ with the stress index. This tells us that the availability of professional help is uncorrelated with state stress, or even oppositely distributed in terms of those geographic areas where it is most needed—that is, to the most stressful areas of the country.

The last two buffering measures are also community-level measures. They deal with different aspects of the integration of communities. Our underlying assumption is that socially integrated communities may be better at coping with the stressful events confronting them than are communities that are more socially disorganized or poorly integrated to begin with.

Percent Voting. This is the percentage of persons eligible to vote who voted in the 1976 national elections. It presumably reflects political alienation or the degree to which citizens feel that they have political efficacy, or the ability to influence events that could affect them.

We found a correlation of $-.58$ $(p < .01)$ between the SSI and the percentage who voted. This is a surprisingly high correlation, but the causal connection, if any, is not immediately clear. One interpretation is that high stress may decrease the citizens' sense of efficacy or be generally demoralizing, which for some manifests itself in not voting. Another interpretation is that states with a high level of social integration and stability have both a high percentage who vote and a low frequency of stressful events.

Welfare Support. This variable is also an indicator of community integration. It is the average monthly payments to families on public assistance. It is an indication of the concern of a community with the welfare of *all* of its citizens, including its least fortunate members and its responsiveness to those in need. This measure is akin to Robert Angell's concept of the "moral integration" of cities (1951), which he and Tropman (1978) operationalized for different cities through the size of total contributions to the Red Feather Campaigns. This variable is also negatively correlated with state stress $(-.24)$. The relationship, although not statistically significant, suggests that people living in more stressful states can count *less* on the support and concern of their neighbors than those living in less stressful areas.

All five of the buffer variables are negatively correlated with state stress levels. There is a certain irony in this pattern in that those populations that are undergoing high stress are the very populations most in need of supportive social arrangements and special resources for coping with that stress. However, the negative correlations suggest that they are less likely to have these special resources and supporting systems than are the populations of the less stressful states.

Endnotes

1. The SSI scores in Figure 3–1 are standardized as ZP scores (Straus, n.d.). ZP scores accomplish two things. First, as with Z scores, they create a variable in which the units have a known meaning (i.e., deviation from the mean). In addition, ZP scoring includes additional calculations that transform the Z score into a score with a mean of 50 and a range of zero to 100. Zero is assigned to cases that are 2.5 or more standard deviations below the mean, and 100 is the ZP score for cases that are 2.5 or more standard deviations above the mean.

   The interpretation of ZP scores can focus on either the fact that each change of one ZP score point is a change of 1 percent of the zero to 100 score range, or focus on the fact that each change of twenty ZP score points is a change of one standard deviation. Thus, statistically trained readers can interpret ZP scores in terms of standard deviations units, and other readers can interpret ZP scores as showing the percentage of the maximum score.

2. A somewhat more precise way to control for age would be age standardization. It was not possible in this case because standardization would require age-specific rates on all of the dependent variables. Age-specific rates are not available for the crime data. Age-specific death rates could be calculated for many of the dependent variables for diseases and other causes of death reported in the *Vital Statistics of the United States,* so that it would be technically possible to standardize that group of dependent variables by age. However, because the number of dependent variables was so large in this study, and because standardization is a cumbersome process that would need to be repeated for each state separately, the task was beyond our resources.

Part Two

THE CORRELATES OF STRESS

Chapter 4

STRESS, CRIME, AND VIOLENCE

Stressful life events (defined as events that require major adaptation) have been implicated in a wide variety of maladaptive behavior and most notably the onset of physical and mental illness for individuals experiencing those events. Several decades of research by physiologists, medical scientists and, more recently, psychologists and sociologists have produced a formidable body of literature to support such a linkage. (For reviews see Dohrenwend and Dohrenwend, 1974; Rabkin and Streuning, 1976; Elliot and Eisdorfer, 1982; Kaplan, 1983.)

Previous Research on Stress and Crime

One of the limitations of that research has been its somewhat single-minded focus on illness and disease as the consequence of stress. In comparison, there has been little sustained research linking stressful life events with criminal and violent behavior as well as some other maladaptive behaviors such as problem drinking and motor vehicle accidents.

The disease and illness emphasis probably stems from the clinical origins of stressful life events research in psychosomatic medicine, a tradition that emphasizes disease states within individuals. While the life events research is no longer the exclusive domain of medical researchers, most of the sociologists and social psychologists who have entered the field more recently have followed in the steps of their predecessors from medical disciplines and focused on mental and physical health consequences of stress.

A review article on the subject of "Stress, Violence and Crime" (Schlesinger and Revitch, 1980) concluded that "most research and theory in the stress field emphasize physiological effects, such as changes in the viscera rather than psychological or behavioral reactions. Violent and criminal behavior is virtually ignored." While that statement refers to stress research in general, it is even more the case with regard to the life events approach to stress. Our examination of the titles of 240 articles employing the life events approach (listed in the *Social Science Citation Index* and elsewhere) found only five articles dealing with crime or criminals. All the others looked at the relation of life events to various physical or mental illnesses or were concerned with issues of measurement, scaling, and so forth.

Most of the literature on the linkage between stress and crime that we have been able to locate deals with stress in general, as opposed to stressful life events. The same review article on stress, violence, and crime (Schlesinger and Revitch, 1980) categorizes as "stress" almost all stimuli stemming from social and situational factors. Such a conception of stress is so diffuse as to make it of little value for systematic research.

A recent effort that has addressed the stress/crime-and-violence connection directly is Molof (1980). Two of the ten papers in that volume related life events to criminal behavior or violence. One of them (also reported in Straus, 1980b) used an abridged version of the Holmes and Rahe Schedule of Recent Life Events to study assault among married couples with a large nationally representative sample. Straus found that the marital assault rate increased as the number of stressors experienced during the year increased. The finding applied to both husbands and wives.

The second study by Petrich and Hart (1980) applied the Holmes and Rahe Schedule of Recent Life Events to the study of criminal behavior and subsequent arrest among three samples drawn from the criminal justice system. (One sample was of juveniles, and two samples were of adult felons, all incarcerated.) The data suggest that "both adult and juvenile criminal behavior, arrest, and incarceration occur in a setting of mounting life change." The prisoners were asked about events during the years prior to imprisonment. This finding is similar to the report of Masuda et al. (1978) in an earlier study of prisoners.

The most extensive study of the relationship of stressful life events to criminal behavior was conducted by Humphrey and

Palmer (1986), with a sample of imprisoned homicide (270) and non-violent property offenders (194). That study measured stress through both recent life events and early stressful events. Those investigators found that lives of criminal homicide offenders are significantly more stressful than those of their non-violent (property) counterparts, and stress tends to be more chronically experienced by homicide offenders. On the other hand, non-violent felonious crime appears to be more a response to "acute, episodic stress than a persistent pattern of stressful events" (Humphrey and Palmer, 1986).

The studies discussed above that use prisoners have methodological limitations which make interpretations difficult. When criminal or violent behavior is measured through arrest, conviction, or sentencing, the nature of the linkage between stress and outcome is unclear. Mounting stress may not increase the propensity to engage in deviant or criminal acts but may only increase the likelihood of getting caught. Thus persons experiencing major life stress may employ less caution than usual in commission of crimes and make dangerous mistakes leading to their detection and arrest. (In a later chapter we employ a parallel explanation to account for the high rate of accidental deaths associated with living in stressful environments—that is, the failure to take usual precautions because of preoccupation with life stressors.)

In our study we use the rates of crimes known to the police. This is a broader, less selective, and therefore more representative measure of incidence of all crimes than data on arrests, crimes brought to trial, conviction, or imprisonment. The latter categories may be more a response to the policies, procedures, and efficiency of the criminal justice system than a reflection of the volume of criminal activities at the community level (see Brenner, 1980b).

When Petrich and Hart (1980) broke the total life events down into separate spheres of activity (family, work, financial, etc.), they found the only type of life event where the incarcerated group reported a greater number of recent stressful experiences than a normative comparison group was "conflict with the law." Thus, the independent variable (life events) and the dependent variable (conviction for crime) were confounded. Thoits (1981) makes this same point in an article about the stress/illness connection. She suggests that the previously well established correlations between undesirable life events and disease may have been inflated due to inclusion of health-related items in the life events checklists. She therefore urges those investigating the relationship between life events and physical illness to use a version of the life events checklist that does not contain health-related events (Thoits, 1981:107).

Our own design avoided this measurement problem. We purposely deleted both legal-criminal types of events and illness, injuries, and hospitalization events from the State Stress Index to avoid possible "self-correlation."

Individual vs. Social System Level Analysis

All of the studies discussed above are at the individual level of analysis. They relate stressful events within the biographies of individuals (or families) to criminal or violent acts by those same persons. However, there are a few studies of the consequences of stressful events in social systems for crimes and violence. Steinberg, Catalano, and Dooley (1981) employed a longitudinal analysis of the rates of reported cases of child maltreatment over a thirty-month period for three different metropolitan areas. They found that an increase in child abuse was preceded by periods of high job loss. They attributed the changes to increased economic stress levels. Brenner (1976, 1980b) has documented in both the United States and in cross-national comparisons strong relationships between unemployment rates and the rates of homicides and other crimes, arrests, convictions, and imprisonments. The relationship prevails for both personal and property crimes.

A limitation of both the Steinberg and the Brenner studies is that community stress is measured only by a single indicator of job loss. Stressful as job loss is, it seems to be much too constricted a measurement of community stress levels.

Studies linking stressful life events to behavioral outcomes such as crimes or violence do not have some of the same methodological handicaps as studies of life events and illness. In the latter case, the research is interested in uncovering the environmental stressors that lead to illness, but the dependent variable, illness, is measured frequently not by actual illness but by care-seeking behavior, such as physicians' visits or hospitalization. This has led some researchers to speculate that mounting life changes result in care-seeking behavior rather than in illness (Mechanic, 1978, 1974). This criticism would apply mainly to disorders of gradual onset and that often go untreated (Rabkin and Streuning, 1976), so that the precipitant to seek help at a particular point becomes the problematic issue. Rabkin and Streuning argue that this particular issue is less relevant with regard to the association of life changes with accidents, suicide, and acute illness because the onset is more clearcut. Their point could be extended to the commission of crimes and violence, since outcomes represent precipitant acts that can more clearly be fixed in time. Further, if death rates for various disorders are used as a "stand-in" for disease onset, there is a substantial but indeterminate lag between stress and the terminal outcome. Again, there is less problem with regard to time lags when dealing with criminal and violent acts.

Theoretical Rationale

Earlier in this chapter we suggested that the paucity of literature on the stress-crime relationship is not accidental. It stems from the origins of stress research, primarily in the areas of psychosomatic medicine and mental health rather than in criminology. However, a number of theoretical approaches do suggest why social stress and crime should be linked (see Brenner, 1980).

Direct Psychological Response to Stress

In the literature on stress and disease, the "fight or flight" concept is prominent (Selye, 1980). When faced with external threats, survival mechanisms that prepare the organism for flight or fight are activated (Cannon, 1963). There is an emergency discharge of adrenalin, a quickening of the pulse, an increase in blood pressure, stimulation of the central nervous system, temporary suspension of digestion, a quickening of blood clotting, and a rise in the blood sugar. Hence the organism is prepared by these physiological responses to engage in physically aggressive or violent activity.

Strength of External Constraints

The process just described is viewed as occurring at a subrational motivational level as a direct psychophysical response to internal stress or tension. However, the response is at the same time severely limited in the case of humans because of various social restraints on behavior. The question then becomes, under what social conditions is physical aggression suppressed and under which conditions is it allowed or even enhanced?

We suspect that under conditions of tight social control and high social cohesion individuals are forced to repress and deny such feelings of aggression toward others in the group. When direct aggression is not an available alternative, the physiological arousal, if continued long enough, may result in structural change in the physiological system (disease); or at the psychological level, aggression may be displaced inward in the form of self-blame, leading to such reactions as clinical depression (Linsky, 1969) or suicide (Straus and Straus, 1953). However, when individuals are not part of such tight relational systems and social control is weak, stress may manifest itself in more direct criminal activities, especially of a more violent and aggressive character for which the physiological state has been prepared.

Culture of Violence

Normative systems may also act as legitimizers of violent activities. According to this approach, differences in level or type of criminal activity or violent behavior may result not so much from the nature of the stress or stimuli as from preexisting response patterns built into the culture of the group and thus into the response repertory of individuals through the existing patterns of socialization. In some societies a larger proportion of people may learn to deal with stress by withdrawal and passivity, while in other societies the proportion responding by the use of aggression may be greater. This idea is consistent with those put forth by Gastil (1971), Glaser (1971), Hackney (1969), and Shannon (1954); these authors report regional differences in several types of deviance. For example, although the rate of property crime is low in the South, the rate of violent crime is high. They attribute these differences to a regional culture pattern that implicitly legitimizes a violent response to personal affronts.

Change and Destabilization

When there are high rates of stressful life events within a community, members are entering and exiting major life statuses and roles. Many of the events included in the SSI represent important role losses and losses of group membership, such as divorce, moving to a different community, becoming unemployed, and dropping out of school. Such losses may not only destabilize individuals but also remove some of the customary informal social controls over their conduct normally exercised by groups. Under such conditions, criminal activity could well be expected to increase.

Tolerance Levels, Law Enforcement, and Reporting of Crimes

Variations in official crime rates reflect not only the true incidence of criminal events but also differences in the reporting of crime. High levels of tension brought on by cumulating stressful events may conceivably lead to decreased tolerance for deviant behavior in a community and increased enforcement and reporting of crime. In an exemplary case study of a series of disorders in English seaside resorts, Stanley Cohen (1980) documents how community tensions, once aroused, encourage police to overreact to relatively minor deviant acts and ironically by so doing actually increase the level of lawlessness in the community.

Thus there are theoretical as well as methodological advantages in extending the analysis of the effects of stress on outcome to the area of crimes and violence.

The Geography of Crime

Although there is a theoretical basis for a macro-sociological study of the relationship between stress and crime, such a study depends on the differences among states being large enough to be worth explaining. The data in the previous chapter show that there are large differences among states in the presence of stressful events. The same should also be true for state-to-state differences in crime for the study to be feasible. Table 4–1a and b therefore presents the rank order of the states in respect to seven major felonies.

State Differences

One obvious fact emerging from Table 4–1a and b is the extreme variation in reported crimes from the highest- to lowest-ranking states. For example, the state of New York, with 529.3 robberies

Rank	Murder, Manslaughter, Per 100K		Forcible Rape Per 100K		Robbery Per 100K		Aggravated Assault Per 100K	
	State	v83	State	v84	State	v85	State	v86
1	ALA	15.1	NEV	47.2	N.Y.	529.3	S.C.	450
2	GA	13.9	ALAS	46.9	MICH	332.6	FLA	415
3	LA	13.2	CAL	44.7	MD	295.5	N.M.	379
4	MISS	12.5	N.M.	41.0	NEV	294.9	ALAS	357
5	TEX	12.2	FLA	36.3	CAL	275.6	CAL	339
6	S.C.	11.6	MICH	36.1	ILL	219.5	NEV	337
7	NEV	11.5	OREG	35.6	MO	204.1	LA	309
8	ALAS	11.3	WASH	34.3	N.J.	200.3	N.C.	306
9	MICH	11.1	COLO	33.8	FLA	186.4	N.Y.	302
10	N.C.	11.1	MD	32.0	OHIO	183.8	MD	297
11	TENN	11.0	S.C.	31.9	MASS	180.2	ARIZ	288
12	N.Y.	10.9	ARIZ	29.7	TENN	147.5	OREG	285
13	FLA	10.7	TEX	29.4	GA	142.4	MICH	266
14	KY	10.6	MO	27.1	COLO	139.7	ALA	256
15	ILL	10.3	OKLA	27.0	TEX	139.0	GA	242
16	CAL	10.3	LA	26.8	PA	138.0	COLO	237
17	ARK	10.1	OHIO	25.8	HAWA	133.0	WASH	231
18	N.M.	9.7	N.Y.	25.8	OREG	132.7	ILL	218
19	VA	9.5	TENN	25.4	ARIZ	129.9	MO	209
20	MO	9.3	GA	24.9	INDI	128.8	TENN	209
21	MD	8.5	WYO	24.9	DEL	128.7	MISS	203
22	ARIZ	7.8	ARK	24.2	ALAS	124.9	R.I.	198
23	OHIO	7.4	HAWA	23.6	N.M.	124.7	MASS	198
24	INDI	7.1	INDI	23.2	LA	124.3	ARK	193
25	WYO	6.9	VA	22.2	CONN	122.9	OKLA	183
26	COLO	6.8	KANS	21.9	WASH	119.5	TEX	175
27	W.VA	6.7	ALA	21.7	VA	108.2	OHIO	172
28	OKLA	6.4	ILL	21.5	S.C.	105.7	N.J.	171
29	HAWA	6.2	UTAH	20.9	KY	98.7	KANS	170
30	DEL	6.2	NEBR	20.5	ALA	96.0	ME	169
31	PA	6.1	N.J.	19.9	R.I.	91.0	DEL	169
32	VT	5.5	IDA	18.7	KANS	85.8	VA	168
33	IDA	5.3	MINN	18.3	MINN	80.4	IDA	163
34	N.J.	5.2	PA	18.1	ARK	76.7	WYO	157
35	MONT	5.0	KY	17.8	N.C.	70.6	INDI	156
36	KANS	4.5	MASS	17.7	OKLA	70.3	S.D.	146
37	UTAH	4.5	DEL	17.7	UTAH	69.4	KY	135
38	WASH	4.3	MISS	16.3	MISS	64.1	PA	133
39	OREG	4.2	S.D.	15.3	NEBR	63.0	CONN	133
40	MASS	3.3	N.C.	15.3	WIS	59.3	UTAH	126
41	N.H.	3.3	VT	14.9	IOWA	41.1	MONT	126
42	CONN	3.1	CONN	14.4	IDA	40.0	NEBR	124
43	WIS	3.0	MONT	13.5	W.VA	38.0	W.VA	97
44	NEBR	2.9	WIS	11.8	ME	37.9	MINN	88
45	ME	2.7	IOWA	10.7	MONT	35.6	VT	80
46	R.I.	2.4	W.VA	10.3	WYO	29.2	IOWA	79
47	IOWA	2.3	ME	9.9	N.H.	24.8	HAWA	67
48	MINN	2.3	N.H.	9.7	S.D.	23.2	WIS	64
49	S.D.	1.7	R.I.	8.5	VT	17.9	N.D.	49
50	N.D.	1.4	N.D.	5.6	N.D.	16.2	N.H.	48

Table 4-1a   Violent Crimes Per 100,000 Population, 1976.

	Burglary Per 100K		Larceny Per 100K		Motor Vehicle Theft Per 100K	
Rank	State	v87	State	v88	State	v89
1	NEV	2392	NEV	4717	MASS	1313
2	ARIZ	2367	ARIZ	4643	R.I.	886
3	CAL	2175	FLA	4074	ALAS	806
4	FLA	1955	COLO	4043	N.Y.	738
5	HAWA	1882	DEL	3916	CAL	644
6	COLO	1880	OREG	3807	MICH	613
7	N.Y.	1764	CAL	3746	CONN	562
8	OREG	1700	HAWA	3669	HAWA	542
9	N.M.	1680	ALAS	3657	N.J.	511
10	MICH	1669	N.M.	3652	ILL	505
11	MASS	1662	MICH	3551	NEV	505
12	WASH	1642	WASH	3414	DEL	484
13	S.C.	1554	UTAH	3302	COLO	442
14	TEX	1548	MD	3242	MD	429
15	DEL	1543	TEX	3209	ARIZ	422
16	N.J.	1504	R.I.	3051	OREG	395
17	GA	1448	ILL	2992	MO	387
18	R.I.	1414	N.J.	2989	OHIO	378
19	MO	1403	OHIO	2978	INDI	372
20	CONN	1384	KANS	2938	TEX	351
21	MD	1360	MONT	2933	WASH	349
22	KANS	1325	IOWA	2885	PA	348
23	TENN	1321	N.Y.	2855	MINN	347
24	OKLA	1317	MO	2795	FLA	340
25	ME	1313	CONN	2786	N.M.	330
26	ALAS	1218	IDA	2777	TENN	326
27	INDI	1216	INDI	2770	GA	320
28	OHIO	1203	WYO	2750	UTAH	317
29	N.C.	1176	WIS	2696	MONT	308
30	ALA	1170	MINN	2673	OKLA	306
31	LA	1141	VA	2650	LA	301
32	UTAH	1138	GA	2618	ALA	262
33	MINN	1122	OKLA	2570	N.H.	252
34	ILL	1090	S.C.	2503	S.C.	251
35	IDA	1037	LA	2447	KY	247
36	VT	1023	MASS	2447	WYO	242
37	VA	1019	NEBR	2434	NEBR	234
38	ARK	937	ME	2337	KANS	232
39	N.H.	937	N.H.	2335	IDA	230
40	KY	930	TENN	2219	VA	226
41	PA	906	N.C.	2124	WIS	223
42	WIS	844	ARK	2014	ME	214
43	MONT	841	ALA	1987	IOWA	207
44	IOWA	827	KY	1858	VT	198
45	MISS	811	VT	1853	N.C.	178
46	WYO	765	N.D.	1805	N.D.	159
47	NEBR	684	PA	1791	ARK	151
48	S.D.	620	S.D.	1684	S.D.	150
49	W.VA	573	W.VA	1459	W.VA	136
50	N.D.	479	MISS	1239	MISS	122

Table 4-1b   Property Crimes Per 100,000 Population, 1976.

per 100,000, has an official rate 32 times greater than the lowest state, North Dakota, with its rate of only 16.2 per 100,000. The rate of reported forcible rapes per 100,100 is 47.2 for Nevada, the highest state, but only 5.6 for North Dakota, which is also lowest on this crime as well. Several previous studies have sought to account for the wide geographical variation in crime rate (Brantingham and Brantingham, 1984; Harries, 1974), although none has been entirely satisfactory. No previous studies have approached the issue from the standpoint of stressful events as an explanatory variable.

There is considerable difference in the state ranking depending on which of the seven crimes are being considered. Alabama leads the nation in homicides per 100,000, followed closely by Georgia, Louisiana, and Mississippi. These are all states of the Southeast and the South Central regions of the country, sometimes known as the Old South. Other high-ranking states in descending order are Texas, South Carolina, Nevada, Alaska, and Michigan. At the other end of the spectrum, the lowest homicide rates are in the Dakotas, Iowa, and Minnesota. The dominance of the South in homicide rates has been noted by many scholars as a long-standing pattern (Gastil, 1971; Harries, 1974; Hackney, 1969; Shannon, 1954). The large black population, lower-status occupations in the South, ruralism, poverty, and southern subjugation have all been cited as explanations (Harries, 1974).

The "culture of violence" theory suggests that the norms in the southern region of the United States either support the use of violence as a method of resolving conflicts or in support of group and individual goals or at least are not strongly condemnatory toward such violence. Other prominent criminologists have argued that the normative or cultural system is insufficient to explain the pattern and that it is the ongoing poverty and blocks to opportunity that lead to higher rates of homicide rather than the cultural past of the region (Loftin and Hill, 1974).

The reported forcible rape rate is highest in Nevada, followed by Alaska, California, and New Mexico. North Dakota is again very low, as are the three New England states of Rhode Island, New Hampshire, and Maine.

The property crimes of burglary and larceny are highest for Nevada and Arizona. For car thefts, however, the highly urban states of Massachusetts and Rhode Island are highest.

Overall, the state of Nevada ranks highest (in the top ten) in six of the seven crimes, while Alaska and Florida are high on five of the seven indexed crimes. Overall, North Dakota is either the lowest state or the next-to-lowest on five of the seven types of crime. In general, the patterns of property crimes are less distinct geographically than are the rates for violent crimes.

Regional Patterns

Geographic differences in reported crime rates are further clarified by Table 4–2, which shows the mean crime rate for each region and division of the country. High rates of forcible rape are predominantly a western pattern (see Baron and Straus, 1986). Highest average rates are reported for the Pacific region (37.0 per 100,000), followed by the mountain states, with a rate of 28.7 per 100,000. In comparison to other regions, New England is particularly low in the incidence of rape (12.5 per 100,000). This regional pattern has been noted by others (Baron and Straus, 1986; Glaser, 1971; Harries, 1974), but like homicide there does not appear to be any simple explanation forthcoming. Explanations for the regional patterns include high male sex ratio, state differences in the status of women (Baron and Straus, 1986), high rates of family problems, and persistance of high rates of deviance in areas formerly part of the frontier of American society (Glaser, 1971).

Aggravated assault, another crime directed against persons, is highest in the South Atlantic region of the country, with a rate of 268.0 per 100,000 population. The Pacific region is also high, with a rate of 259.8. The West North Central states are low in assault rates. Again, this pattern of aggravated assault follows largely the same geographic distribution as does the homicide rate and is undoubtedly responsive to some of the same causal conditions.

The property crimes of both burglary and larceny again show highest rates of reported crimes in the Pacific and Mountain states in that order. Lowest rates of burglary are found in the West North Central states, while lowest rates of larceny are found in the East South Central states.

The regional pattern of motor vehicle thefts is quite different from the pattern of the other two property crimes. Here, New England leads the country with a rate of 570.8 per 100,000 persons. The Pacific region is second in this case, with a rate of

State Characteristic	Year	Region			
		North East	North Central	South	West
Crime: Murder, Manslaughter per 100K v83 ###	76	4.7	5.3	10.6	7.2
Crime: Forcible Rape per 100K v84 ###	76	15.4	19.8	23.7	31.9
Crime: Robbery per 100K v85	76	149.1	119.8	118.3	126.9
Crime: Aggravated Assault per 100K v86 #	76	159.1	145.1	237.9	237.9

#=p<.05, ##=p<.01, ###=p<.001

Table 4-2   Regional Differences in Crime.

547.2. Fewest car thefts are reported in the East South Central region.

Intercorrelations of Crime Variables

The rankings and the regional differences just examined show a tendency for some states and regions to be high in respect to more than one type of crime. To obtain more specific information on this question, we computed the correlation of each of the crimes with the others, as shown in Table 4–3.

There is considerable intercorrelation of the rates of different types of crimes with one another by state. The correlations are for the most part in the moderate to high range—twelve out of the twenty-one are .50 or higher. However, some, such as between homicide and motor vehicle theft, approach zero. The highest correlation is between burglary and larceny (.80).

The correlations suggest that there are underlying similarities, but the variables are far from isomorphic. In only two of the twenty-one correlations between pairs of variables do they explain as much as half of the total variation in the other variable. This pattern supports the value of using all seven crime indicators. If all should be correlated with the State Stress Index, it would be

	Homi-cide	Rape	Rob-bery	Assault	Burg-lary	Lar-ceny
Homicide v83	1.0					
Forcible Rape v84	.54	1.0				
Robbery v85	.43	.54	1.0			
Aggravated Assault v86	.64	.77	.51	1.0		
Burglary v87	.30	.68	.61	.62	1.0	
Larceny v88	.08	.67	.44	.45	.80	1.0
Motor Vehicle Theft v89	-.01	.28	.56	.26	.52	.42

All correlations are significant at p<=.05 except the correlations of homicide with larceny and motor vehicle theft.

Table 4-3   Intercorrelations of UCR Crime Variables (N = 50).

strong evidence for the importance of our stress index in explaining this broad range of criminal behavior.

Social Stress and Crime

Stressful life events are positively correlated with all seven of the so-called "index crimes." That is, the higher the state stress level, the higher the crime rates for these states (see Table 4–4). Six of seven correlations are statistically significant at the $p < .01$ or better. It is unlikely that the consistent correlations of this magnitude could have arisen simply because the seven crime variables are themselves highly correlated, since we have already seen that there is not that much overlap between the crime variables. The alternative explanation, which seems to fit the data better, is that cumulative stressful events are causally related to each of these crimes.

The findings apply to both violent and property crimes. But violent crimes on the average are most strongly associated with high levels of stressful events in the community. The correlations with violent crimes range from a low at .45 for robbery to a high of .72 for rape. Robbery, although officially classified as a violent crime, is more closely related to the property crimes in that it

Crime	Correlation With Stress Index (tx15)
A. VIOLENT CRIMES	
Murder, Manslaughter v83	.69***
Forcible Rape v84	.72***
Robbery v85	.45**
Aggravated Assault v86	.68***
B. PROPERTY CRIMES	
Burglary v87	.60***
Larceny v88	.41**
Motor Vehicle Theft v89	.20

**=p<.01, ***=p<.001

Table 4-4 Correlations of the State Stress Index with Violent and Property Crime Rates (N = 50 States).

represents more instrumental behavior than other violent crimes. The other three more purely violent crimes have correlations of .68 (aggravated assault), .69 (murder, manslaughter), and .72 (forcible rape).

The correlations with property crimes as a group are not as highly associated on average with state stress as are the violent crimes, but two of the three correlations are still significant at the .01 level (larceny and burglary). The average of the three correlations of stress with property crime is .40, compared to an average correlation of .63 for the relation between the State Stress Index and the four violent crimes. This means that the stressfulness of life in the states, as measured by the stress index, is associated with 40 percent of the state-to-state differences in violent crimes but only 16 percent of the differences in property crimes. Since violent crimes represent behavior motivations more by expressive rather than instrumental goals, the finding of higher correlations with violent crimes is consistent with the psychophysical arousal model of stress discussed earlier.

We are not, of course, suggesting that arousal brought on by mounting stress leads inevitably to violence. A later chapter considers the question of the circumstances under which stress leads to one particular type of response or another. We consider the cultural context of states within which stress operates as one of the determinants of the directionality of stress-connected behavior.

Net and Interactive Effects of Stress on Crime

Control for Spurious Relationships

In the preceding section we examined the simple correlations of the State Stress Index with variation in crime rates. One possibility worth considering is that the correlations with crime and violence may be partially or wholly spurious. A study of the frequency of life events in different populations by Masuda and Holmes (1978) revealed that young persons (under thirty) have higher frequencies of life events and perceive those events as more stressful than persons over thirty years. Crime rates from most types of crimes are also highest for younger populations. Therefore, a state with a younger population could well experience both higher levels of stressful life events and crimes without any direct causal connection between the two.

We believe several other factors could also have contributed to spurious correlations because they are plausibly related to both crime and stressful events. These are (1) the percentage of a state's population with four years of high school, (2) the percentage below the poverty line, (3) the percentage black, and (4) the percentage living in metropolitan areas.

The overlap or "confounding" of the stress and crime data with other variables can be controlled through the use of multiple regression. We therefore carried out a multiple regression analysis to relate the State Stress Index to the dependent variables, and we also included these four control variables. This permits examination of the effect of state stress on the dependent variable, with effect of the control variables statistically removed. The equation also shows the net effect of each control variable on crime. This provides a useful standard for comparing the magnitude of the state stress effects versus the magnitude of the effects of the control variables.

Buffer Variables and Interactive Effects

Most recent theoretical models of stress have developed beyond
the simple evaluation of the effects of stressor events on maladaptive behavior that characterized much of the earlier work. This
development has been prompted in part by the fact that correlations between stressful events and outcomes such as illness and
maladaptive behavior have as a general rule been low, although
stable. One important direction in attempts to identify a model
that explains more of the variations on maladaptive behavior has
been a search for mediating variables, especially "buffering" conditions that serve to protect or buffer persons from the more
debilitating consequences of exposure to stressful events.

At the individual level these buffer variables include a wide
range of coping skills and personal resources which serve to make
events and changes less stressful than they might otherwise be or
to facilitate successful adaptation to such events. These buffers
include personal, material, and social resources. The concept of
social support, for example, has been examined extensively as a
major mediator between stressful events and physical or mental
illness (Lin et al., 1979; Gore, 1981; Turner, 1981), although the
validity of the social support hypothesis is still an open question
(Thoits, 1982). Social support is often indicated by the accessibility
of other people who can or do either provide for the emotional
needs of the person or provide more instrumental help.

We suggest that communities vary in their capacities to withstand stressors in a manner somewhat parallel to that of individuals. Some communities are endowed with a greater store of
available resources to help their members to adapt to stressful
conditions, and some have more extensive helping networks of
institutions and organizations for assisting those with problems or
are more responsive to those in need than are other communities.
These issues have at least as much relevance, if not more, at the
community or state level. Can high levels of stress within communities be offset or alleviated in whole or in part by community
institutions and resources for combating stress?

In Chapter 3 the five buffer variables used in this study were
described and discussed. In brief, they are as follows:

1. "Family integration," as measured by an index reflecting the
   proportion of the population who are living with close rela-

tives in common households as opposed to living alone or in more personally isolated circumstances.

2. "Educational resources," as measured by the percentage of adults who have completed high school or higher.
3. "Mental health support," as measured by an index composed of the number of psychiatrists, clinical psychologists and psychiatric social workers resident in the state, per 100,000 population.
4. "Political integration," as measured by the percentage of the voting age population who voted in 1976.
5. An additional aspect of social integration, as measured by public assistance generosity.

These buffering variables were entered into the regression equation in a manner consistent with our theoretical concerns— that is, as interaction terms. There is, however, a second way in which these buffering variables are relevant. Several of them may directly affect crime or the other outcome variables in the study on their own—over and above any "interaction effects" that may be present. Indeed, some researchers have argued that variables such as "social support" have a more important role as direct causal agents than as buffers (Thoits, 1982). To allow for this possibility, we also entered the five buffers as dummy variables in the equation so that we can view their direct effects as well.

Stress and Violent Crime

Homicide. The multiple regression analysis in Table 4–5 confirms the simple correlation analysis in showing that state-to-state differences in the number of stressor events are positively associated with state differences in the murder and manslaughter rate. Specifically, the regression coefficient indicates that for each increase of one point of the State Stress Index (the index varies from 16 to 100 with a theoretical minimum and maximum of 0 and 100), there is an average increase of .2 murders per 100,000 population.

This regression coefficient indicates a much stronger association between stress and murder than .2 might suggest. This is because one has to judge the .2 in relation to the average murder rate for all states—7.38 in 1976.[1] One can think of a regression coefficient of .2 as showing that an increase of just a single point on the stress scale

Independent Variables	Regression Coefficient	t	p<
State Stress Index (tx15)	.20	4.80	.001
Buffer Variables:			
% Of Voters Who Voted (v706)	-1.97	2.96	.01
Controls:			
% Black (v750)	.14	3.55	.001
Multiple R squared = .78			

Table 4-5   Regression of Murder/Manslaughter Rate Per 100,000 (v83) on Stress, Buffering, and Control Variables (N = 50 States).

is associated with an average increase in murder amounting to 2.7 percent of the average state murder rate; and an increase of ten stress points is associated with an average increase of 27 percent of the average state murder rate. Moreover, it is important to remember that this coefficient is not due to confounding with any of the other fourteen variables originally entered into the regression equation (four control variables, five buffer variables, and five stress-by-buffer-interaction-effect variables).

Of the four control variables, only the Percent Black has a statistically significant effect on murder. For every 1 percent increase in a state's black population, there is a corresponding increase of .14 murders per 100,000.

None of the five stress-by-buffer interaction variables was statistically significant. Consequently, we find no evidence that these buffer variables operated to moderate the relation of stressful events to murder. However, one of the buffer variables—the percentage of the voting age population who voted in 1976—shows a significant main effect on the murder rate. For every increase of 1 percent in number of eligible persons voting, there was an average *decrease* of 1.97 in the numbers of murders per 100,000 population.

The adjusted R square of .78 indicates that a very large proportion of the total variance in the rate of murder/manslaughter is explained by the variables included in the equation.

Rape.   The simple correlation of the state stress and the number of rapes per 100,000 was shown in the previous section to be

Independent Variable	Regression Coefficient	t	p<
A. RAPE (v84) Multiple R square = .72			
State Stress Index (tx15)	.93	6.93	.001
Buffer Variables:			
% Of Voters who Voted (v706)	-6.54	3.01	.01
Controls:			
% Population Age 15-24 (p5r2)	2.53	3.47	.01
B. ROBBERY (v85) Multiple R squared = .55			
State Stress Index (tx15)	3.60	2.33	.02
Controls:			
% Population in Metro Areas (v206)	1.80	3.65	.001
C. AGGRAVATED ASSAULT (v86) Multiple R squared = .47			
State Stress Index (tx15)	7.39	4.63	.001

Table 4-6 Regression of Rape, Robbery, and Assault Rates on Stress, Buffering, and Control Variables (N = 50 States).

extremely high (.72). The first regression coefficient in Table 4–6 of .93 indicates that for each increase of one point in the State Stress Index, there is an average increase of almost one rape per 100,000 population. That coefficient is significant beyond the .001 level.

One of the buffer variables—the percentage of those eligible to vote who voted—is also significantly related to the rape rate. This variable was included in the analysis as a proxy for political integration. Since this variable was dichotomized at the median, the regression coefficient of − 6.54 means that, after controlling for the other five variables in the equation, there is an average of 6.54 fewer rapes per 100,000 in states that are above the median in the number of voters voting in comparison to states that are below the median in this regard. In this case, the measure of "political integration" has a "direct effect" on the dependent variable (rape) rather than as a mediating factor influencing the stress-rape relationship.

The last row of section A in Table 4–6 reveals that one of the control variables—Population 15- to 24—shows a significant regression coefficient with the rate of rape. The larger the percentage of 15- to 24-year-olds in the population of a state, the higher the rape rate. In fact, each 1 percent increase in the population of this age is associated with an average increase of two and a half additional rapes per 100,000 population.

Finally, the combination of the stress buffer and control variables shown in Table 4–6 as independent variables results in an adjusted multiple R squared of .76. This indicates that over three-fourths of the state-to-state variance in rape rates is associated with the variables listed in section A of Table 4–6.

Robbery.   The results in section B of Table 4–6 indicate that robbery also is significantly related to the State Stress Index, but in this case there are no significant main effects or interaction effects for any of the buffering variables. The regression coefficient shows that for every increase of one point on the SSI, there is a corresponding average increase of 3.6 robberies per 100,000 population.

The only one of the control variables significantly related to stress is the percentage of the population living in metropolitan areas. The regression coefficient indicates that for every 1 percent increase in population living in metropolitan areas, there is an average increase of 1.8 robberies per 100,000. This result is highly significant, as shown by a t of 3.65 and a p of $< .001$. Altogether, the fifteen variables in the model accounted for slightly over half of the state-by-state variance in the number of robberies per 100,000 population.

Aggravated Assault.   The results for aggravated assault in section C of Table 4–6 show there is a significant effect for stress but for none of the other fifteen variables in the model. The regression coefficient of 7.39 shows that for every one point increase in the stress score, there is an average increase of more than seven assaults per 100,000 population. This relationship is net of all other relationships in the equation and is highly significant as indicated by the t of 4.6. Since assault is one of the most violent and expressive of the various crimes considered, its singular linkage with stress is consistent with the physiological arousal model discussed earlier in this chapter.

Summary for Violent Crimes. The regression coefficients in Tables 4–5 and 4–6 indicate that the level of stress characteristic of each state is positively related to all four forms of violent crimes examined in this study: homicide, rape, robbery, and assault. As stressful life events increase in states, so on the average do the rates for homicide, rape, robbery, and assault. These relationships were in every case statistically significant. Further, they do not appear to be spurious, since the stress/violence relationship was tested using a model in which the effects of four possible confounding variables, five buffering variables, and five interactions were controlled.

Some of the "control" variables are also strongly related to violent crime, but none are as consistently or as significantly related as the state stress variable.

The adjusted multiple R squared for the four violent crimes is comparatively high, ranging from .47 for assault to a high of .76 for rape. This suggests that the model includes appropriate and important variables in explaining state-by-state differences in violent crimes.

No support was observed for the buffering hypothesis at least as far as violence was involved. There were no significant interactions involving stress and any of the five potential buffering variables.

Stress and Property Crime

Burglary. State-to-state differences in stressor events are positively associated with the burglary rate (Table 4–7). For every increase of one unit in the State Stress Index, there is an average increase of thirty-two burglaries per 100,000. This result is net of the four control variables and is highly significant ($t = 5.13$; $p <$ .001).

The regression coefficients for two of the control variables (percent of persons living in metropolitan areas and the Percent Black) are also significantly associated with the rate of burglary. For every 1 percent increase in the state population living in metropolitan areas, there is a corresponding average increase of 10.5 burglaries per 100,000 population. The Percent Black has an opposite relation to burglary: For every increase of 1 percent of

Independent Variable	Regression Coefficient	t	p<
A. BURGLARY (v87) **Multiple R squared = .62**			
State Stress Index (tx15)	31.88	5.13	.001
Controls:			
% Population in Metro Areas (v206)	10.50	5.28	.001
% Black (v750)	-17.41	2.83	.01
B. LARCENY (v88) **Multiple R squared = .64**			
State Stress Index:			
When Public Assistance is Low	55.40	5.13	.001
When Public Assistance is High	48.44	*	
Controls:			
% Population Age 15-24 (p5r2)	215.98	3.60	.001
% Population in Metro Areas (v206)	13.74	4.01	.001
% Black (v750)	-33.84	3.18	.01
C. MOTOR VEHICLE THEFT (v89) **Multiple R squared = .46**			
State Stress Index (tx15)	4.48	1.17	.25
Controls:			
% Population in Metro Areas (v206)	4.60	3.76	.001

* t = 2.07 (p<.05) for the significance of the difference between the Stress-Larceny relationship when public assistance is low (as given by the regression coefficient in the previous row) versus the Stress-Larceny relationship when public assistance is high (this row). The value for the high public assistance row was obtained by computing a regression coefficient for the interaction of stress with public assistance (b2 in the following equation):

$$y = a + b1*x1 + b2*x2 + b3*x3 + b4*x4 + b5*x5$$

Where: x1 = State Stress Index, x2 = x1*d and d = public assistance converted to a dummy variable by coding states above the median as 1, and states below the median as 0, x3 = % of population age 15-24, x4 = % of population in metropolitan areas, x5 = % black.

The value of b2 in this equation is -6.96. Thus, when public assistance was high, the effect of stress on larceny was <u>decreased</u> by 6.96 larcenies, i.e., from an average of 55.40 additional larcenies per 100,000 for each additional point on the stress index, to 48.44 larcenies for each increase of one point on the stress index.

Table 4-7 Regression of Burglary, Larceny, and Motor Vehicle Theft Rates on Stress, Buffering, and Control Variables (N = 50 States).

blacks in a state population, there is an average *decrease* of 17.41 burglaries per 100,000 population ($t = 2.83$; $p < .01$).

Almost two-thirds of the total variance in state-by-state burglary rates are explained by stress in combination with the other variables in the model (adjusted R squared $= .62$).

Larceny. State stress is strongly associated with differences between states in the rate of larceny. The regression coefficient of 55.40 indicates that for every increase of one point in the State Stress Index, there is an increase of 55 larcenies per 100,000 population.

There is also a significant interaction with one of the buffering variables—level of public assistance support. The relationship between stress and crime is significantly weaker (48.4) when public assistance generosity is low. Thus, public assistance generosity, used here as a measure of community concern and integration, appears to mediate the stress-crime relationship in the direction suggested by the buffering hypothesis. Interestingly, the buffering variable involves financial support, perhaps making it especially relevant to financially motivated crime such as larceny. Larceny includes such acts as shoplifting, purse snatching, bicycle theft, and theft from motor vehicles, which are primarily crimes of poor persons.

There are also significant regression coefficients between three different control variables and larceny. For every increase of 1 percent in the population 15 to 24, there is an average increase of 216 larcenies per 100,000. For every 1 percent increase in population resident in SMSA's, there is an average increase of 14 larcenies per 100,000. Finally, for every 1 percent increase in the percentage of blacks in the population, there are 34 *fewer* larcenies per 100,000. At first glance, the negative association of Percent Black and both larceny and burglary seems counterintuitive, because at the individual level arrest rates for burglary are higher among blacks than whites. However, several of the states with higher percentages of blacks include relatively rural southern states which have overall low burglary and larceny rates, probably related to their rurality. Approximately two-thirds of the total variance in larceny rates is explained by the variables in the equation.

Motor Vehicle Theft. State stress is positively associated with motor vehicle theft, but the regression coefficient of 4.48 fails to be significant. The only significant regression coefficient is for the percentage of the population living in metropolitan areas. For every 1 percent increase in populations living in metropolitan areas, there is an average increase of four car thefts per 100,000 population.

Explanations of the Stress-Crime Relationship

The findings in this chapter have demonstrated considerable evidence that the crime rates for states are consistently correlated with our measure of state stress levels. This generalization holds for both violent crimes and property crimes, although the relationship is, on average, stronger for the crimes of violence.

The strength and consistency of the findings is surprising in view of the fact that most life events research has focused on illness rather than on crime. These findings provide considerable support for the idea that there is a relationship between social stress and crime. However, the findings leave important issues unresolved. Specifically, our earlier discussion raised the question of the possible explanations for a linkage between stress and crime, but the current research was not designed to test the merits of the different explanations. These findings suggest that more attention needs to be paid to understanding the intervening processes that underly the stress-crime relationship.

Endnote

1. The overall U.S. murder rate was 8.8 that year. However, the average of the fifty state rates is lower because the large states tend to have high murder rates and this strongly influences the overall U.S. rate.

Chapter 5

STRESS, MALADAPTIVE BEHAVIOR, AND DISEASE

Reactions to stress include a very broad array of human troubles. The previous chapter showed considerable linkage between the stressfulness of life in different states and crime rates. This chapter deals with two other types of stress-related outcomes. The first half of the chapter is concerned with a number of maladaptive behaviors and the second half with different types of disease.

Maladaptive Behavior

The term *maladaptive behavior* is a somewhat broadly defined category. It groups several potential responses to stress, all of which involve behaviors that are detrimental to health or even survival. We include indicators of the following problems:

1. *Accidents*. Accidents of various kinds result from engaging in hazardous behavior or failing to take proper precautions or avoiding dangerous situations. Edward Suchman (1970) suggests that accidents should be considered as social pathology—an indication of disorder in particular social systems. Evidence also suggests that many auto accident deaths should be regarded as suicides (Phillips, 1977).
2. *Alcoholism*. The relative prevalence of alcoholism in the states will be measured by the death rate for cirrhosis of the liver (Hyman et al., 1980).
3. *Heavy Smoking*. The occurrence of malignant neoplasm of the respiratory system has been closely linked to smoking

behavior, at least since the "Surgeon General's Report on
Smoking and Health" (Public Health Service, 1964).
4. *Suicide*. Suicide, of course, is the ultimate self-destructive
behavior and has long been considered as a sensitive indicator of problems within social systems (Durkheim, 1951).

Each of those maladaptive behaviors involves actions that produce serious disease states such as lung cancer or cirrhosis, life-
threatening conditions such as automobile crashes, or attempts to
take one's own life.

The criminal behaviors reported in the previous chapter may
also involve such risks. However, we found it useful to separate
these maladaptive behaviors from crimes on the grounds that
criminal acts are broadly assumed to have a different motivational
basis in Western jurisprudence than the various self-inflicted
maladies that we have grouped under "maladaptive behaviors."
Maladaptive behaviors are also distinguished somewhat from the
several diseases discussed in the second half of this chapter, since
there is no clear behavioral activity in the latter case intervening
between stress and disease states.

Geographic Distribution of Maladaptive Behaviors

Table 5–1a and b shows the rank order of the states in respect to
maladaptive behaviors, and Table 5–2 describes the regional differences in the rates of these maladaptive behaviors. Regional differences are as sharp here as in the case of stressful events and in the
rate of criminal activities in the previous chapter. For example,
Figure 5–1 graphs the data on the rate of motor vehicle accident
deaths from the first two rows of Table 5–2. It shows that automobile accident deaths are highest in the western states (34.3 per
100,000), followed by the South (27.8 per 100,000). In sharp
contrast, the North East had only 16.9 deaths per 100,000 from
motor vehicle accidents.

Deaths from industrial accidents (third row of Table 5–2) show a
similar pattern. The western states are the most dangerous area
(3.7 deaths per 100,000) of the country, and the North East is again
the safest region (1.8).

The cirrhosis-of-the-liver row of Table 5–2 also shows strong
regional differences in this indicator of heavy drinking and alcoholism. Since different states and regions have different ethnic and

	Motor Vehicle Accidents: Deaths Per 100K		Industrial Accidents: Deaths Per 100K		Accidents: Deaths Per 100K	
Rank	State	t156r	State	t161r	State	t151r
1	WYO	53.4	ALAS	6.3	ALAS	115.3
2	N.M.	48.7	IDA	6.2	WYO	92.0
3	MONT	39.8	S.D.	5.9	N.M.	78.9
4	ARIZ	39.3	LA	4.9	IDA	76.6
5	IDA	37.9	MONT	4.9	MONT	76.4
6	NEV	36.4	WYO	4.7	NEV	69.5
7	ALAS	35.6	W.VA	4.7	ALA	68.6
8	ALA	34.6	N.D.	4.6	ARIZ	68.0
9	S.C.	34.2	KY	4.6	MISS	67.2
10	OKLA	33.5	OREG	4.4	S.D.	66.0
11	MISS	32.6	OKLA	4.3	S.C.	64.9
12	S.D.	31.8	IOWA	3.8	LA	64.5
13	N.D.	30.7	MISS	3.8	KY	63.5
14	OREG	29.6	ALA	3.8	OKLA	63.0
15	GA	29.6	KANS	3.7	GA	61.9
16	TENN	29.4	WASH	3.5	N.D.	61.8
17	TEX	29.4	TEX	3.5	OREG	60.0
18	LA	28.5	NEBR	3.4	W.VA	59.1
19	WASH	28.2	NEV	3.3	TENN	58.8
20	W.VA	28.0	ARK	3.2	WASH	57.7
21	KY	27.9	VT	3.2	N.C.	57.6
22	COLO	27.8	UTAH	3.1	TEX	56.0
23	UTAH	27.2	GA	3.1	ARK	56.0
24	N.C.	26.7	TENN	3.1	COLO	54.5
25	KANS	26.3	INDI	2.9	KANS	53.5
26	ARK	25.8	VA	2.9	VA	52.9
27	MO	25.2	ME	2.8	UTAH	52.8
28	CAL	25.1	MO	2.8	MO	52.7
29	INDI	24.7	S.C.	2.8	NEBR	51.8
30	NEBR	24.3	MINN	2.7	CAL	49.6
31	VA	24.2	ARIZ	2.5	INDI	49.4
32	FLA	23.6	COLO	2.5	FLA	48.2
33	IOWA	23.2	WIS	2.5	MINN	47.4
34	MINN	22.8	MICH	2.4	IOWA	46.9
35	MICH	22.0	DEL	2.2	VT	46.4
36	VT	21.5	N.M.	2.2	ILL	43.6
37	WIS	20.7	N.C.	2.1	MICH	43.5
38	ILL	20.2	PA	2.1	PA	42.7
39	DEL	19.9	OHIO	2.1	ME	41.8
40	N.H.	18.4	ILL	2.0	DEL	41.6
41	PA	18.4	N.H.	1.8	WIS	41.4
42	ME	18.0	FLA	1.8	OHIO	40.4
43	OHIO	17.5	CAL	1.6	N.H.	39.7
44	R.I.	17.4	MD	1.6	R.I.	39.3
45	HAWA	16.9	R.I.	1.6	MD	37.6
46	MD	16.8	HAWA	1.5	MASS	36.8
47	CONN	15.1	N.Y.	1.1	N.J.	34.1
48	N.J.	14.9	CONN	1.1	N.Y.	32.1
49	MASS	14.2	N.J.	1.0	CONN	31.5
50	N.Y.	13.8	MASS	0.9	HAWA	31.2

Table 5-1a   Accident Death Rates Per 100,000 Population, 1976.

Rank	Suicide: Deaths Per 100K State	t391r	Total Cirrhosis Deaths Per 1 Million State	z185	Mal. Neoplasm: Resp. System: Deaths Per 100K State	t91r
1	NEV	86.0	NEV	323.9	FLA	65.2
2	ALAS	67.5	N.Y.	270.3	R.I.	55.5
3	COLO	56.0	CAL	255.4	W.VA	53.6
4	ARIZ	55.8	FLA	248.0	OKLA	53.3
5	N.M.	55.5	DEL	229.3	KY	52.7
6	CAL	54.7	R.I.	227.5	NEV	50.9
7	FLA	53.1	N.M.	218.4	DEL	50.6
8	WYO	52.3	MASS	214.1	ARK	49.6
9	MONT	51.4	N.J.	213.4	ME	48.8
10	IDA	49.5	MICH	212.9	N.H.	48.8
11	VA	48.1	ARIZ	206.1	TENN	48.5
12	OREG	48.0	ILL	203.7	N.J.	48.4
13	VT	47.7	N.H.	197.8	MO	48.1
14	WASH	44.9	ME	194.9	VT	47.7
15	GA	44.0	OREG	190.8	PA	47.4
16	OKLA	43.4	WASH	190.4	N.Y.	47.3
17	N.H.	41.6	MD	190.2	LA	47.3
18	KY	40.7	W.VA	189.6	WASH	47.0
19	TENN	40.7	ALAS	188.7	OREG	46.9
20	UTAH	40.1	CONN	186.8	OHIO	46.9
21	TEX	39.9	PA	186.6	ALA	46.8
22	N.C.	39.7	N.C.	171.6	MISS	45.7
23	MICH	39.6	WYO	169.5	MD	45.6
24	R.I.	38.6	OHIO	169.1	ILL	45.2
25	OHIO	38.4	MONT	164.9	CONN	44.9
26	MO	38.2	OKLA	162.0	MASS	44.7
27	ME	38.1	VA	158.1	INDI	44.4
28	KANS	38.1	GA	155.7	CAL	44.3
29	WIS	38.0	VT	155.0	KANS	43.1
30	DEL	37.6	S.D.	152.8	VA	42.3
31	LA	37.0	TEX	150.1	MICH	42.0
32	MD	35.3	COLO	149.5	TEX	41.1
33	INDI	35.3	WIS	147.4	NEBR	41.0
34	PA	35.2	LA	145.2	GA	40.7
35	IOWA	34.3	S.C.	143.4	IOWA	40.3
36	S.C.	34.2	MO	140.3	ARIZ	40.0
37	W.VA	33.8	KY	135.5	N.C.	39.1
38	MINN	33.5	NEBR	134.9	S.C.	38.5
39	ARK	33.3	INDI	134.9	S.D.	37.6
40	HAWA	33.1	IDA	128.7	MONT	37.3
41	S.D.	32.4	MINN	126.4	WYO	37.2
42	N.D.	32.3	UTAH	125.6	WIS	36.4
43	ALA	32.2	ALA	123.3	MINN	34.0
44	NEBR	30.9	IOWA	123.3	IDA	31.5
45	MISS	30.0	N.D.	123.0	HAWA	28.2
46	CONN	29.2	TENN	122.5	COLO	26.9
47	ILL	29.1	KANS	118.3	N.D.	26.4
48	MASS	28.2	HAWA	110.7	N.M.	26.0
49	N.Y.	26.9	MISS	106.8	ALAS	19.1
50	N.J.	23.9	ARK	106.1	UTAH	14.9

Table 5-1b   Cirrhosis, Respiratory Neoplasm, and Suicide Death Rates, 1976.

Mean for Each Census Region (1st Row) and Division (2nd Row)

State Characteristic	N. East		N. Central		South			West		ANOVA F*
	NE	MA	ENC	WNC	SA	ESC	WSC	MT	PA	
Motor Veh. Accdnts: Deaths per 100K (t156r) — Region	16.9		24.2			27.8		34.3		14.71***
— Division	17.5	15.7	21.1	26.4	25.4	31.2	29.3	38.9	27.1	10.13***
Industrial Accdnts: Deaths per 100K (t161r) — Region	1.8		3.3			3.3		3.7		4.85**
— Division	1.9	1.5	2.4	3.9	2.7	3.9	4.0	3.7	3.5	3.29**
Accidents: Deaths per 100K (t151r) — Region	38.3		49.9			57.6		67.9		10.54***
— Division	39.3	36.3	43.7	54.3	53.0	64.6	59.9	71.1	62.8	4.79***
Total Cirrhosis Deaths per 1 Million (z185) — Region	205.2		149.0			158.6		186.4		4.03*
— Division	196.1	223.5	173.6	131.3	185.8	122.1	140.9	185.9	187.3	3.30**
Mal. Neo: Resp. Syst: Deaths per 100K (t91r) — Region	48.2		40.5			47.6		34.7		8.79***
— Division	48.5	47.8	43.0	38.7	47.0	48.5	47.9	33.1	37.1	3.29**
Suicide: Deaths per 100K (t391r) — Region	34.4		35.1			39.0		53.5		14.02***
— Division	37.3	28.7	36.1	34.3	40.8	36.0	38.4	55.9	49.7	5.85***

*=p<.05, **=p<.01, ***=p<.001 with 1 and 8 df.

NE = New England: CN, MA, NH, VT, ME, RI; MA = Middle Atlantic: NY, NJ, PA; ENC = East North Central: OH, IN, IL, MI, WI; WNC = West North Central: MN, IA, MO, ND, SD, NE, KS; SA = South Atlantic: DE, MD, DC, VA, WV, NC, SC, GA, FL; ESC = East South Central: KY, TN, AL, MS; WSC = West South Central: AR, LA, OK, TX; MT = Mountain: MT, ID, WY, CO, NM, AZ, UT, NV; PA = Pacific: WA, OR, CA, AK, HI

Table 5-2   Indicators of Maladaptive Behavior by Census Region and Division.

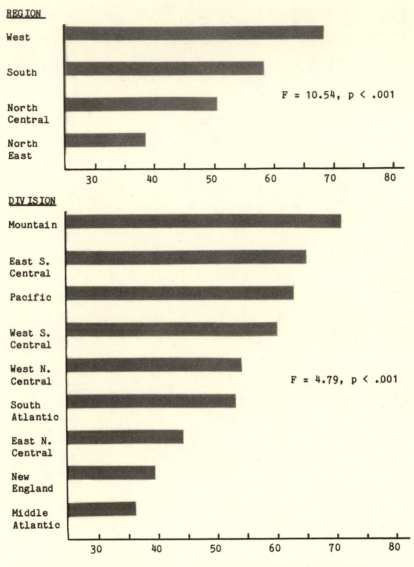

Figure 5-1   Accidental Death Rate Per 100,000 Population, 1976

religious compositions and different prohibitionist histories, it is not surprising to find major variations from one state to another and one region to another in cirrhosis deaths. Highest rates of cirrhosis deaths occurred in the north eastern states (205 per million population), followed by the states of the West (186). The north-central states (149) and the South (158) were lowest in the cirrhosis death rate.

When we look at individual states (see Table 5–1b), it is the states of Nevada (324), New York (270), and California (255) that lead the country in cirrhosis death rates per 100,000 and, presumably, alcohol problems. Arkansas (106), Mississippi (107), and Hawaii (111) have comparatively low death rates for cirrhosis of the liver.

Respiratory cancer, our indicator of heavy smoking, is highest in the north east states (48.2) and the South (47.6 per 100,000). Lowest rates are registered in the West (34.7). Among individual states, Florida (65 per 100,000), Rhode Island (56), and West Virginia (54) show the highest rates of respiratory cancer, while Utah is lowest, with only 15 deaths per 100,000 population. Other factors besides smoking behavior could play a part in mortality attributed to respiratory cancer as suggested by high rates for Rhode Island, which has considerable textile manufacturing, and West Virginia, with its coal-mining industry. However, the extreme position occupied by the Mormon state of Utah (lowest) would seem to validate the mortality rate as sensitive to smoking intensity. (See also the correlations in Linsky, Colby, and Straus, 1986b.)

The last row of Table 5–2 shows that the suicide rate is highest in the western states (53.5 per 100,000 population). No other region is close in magnitude of the suicide rate. Residents of the North East are the least suicide-prone of any regional population (34.4 per 100,000 population). Among individual states, Nevada (86 per 100,000) and Alaska (67) have the most suicide-prone populations. New Jersey (24) and New York (27) have the least suicidal populations.

Correlation of Maladaptive Behavior with Social Stress

Table 5–3 presents the simple correlations between the State Stress Index and the six dependent variables discussed above. The

Cause of Death	Correlation	p<
Accidental Death Rate		
Total (t151r)	.35	.01
Males (t366r)	.34	.01
Females (t367r)	.38	.01
Motor Vehicle Death Rates		
Total (t156r)	.27	.05
Males (t370r)	.26	.05
Females (t371r)	.28	.05
Indust. Accidents Death Rates		
Total (t161r)	.05	N.S.
Males (t374r)	.05	N.S.
Females (t375r)	.04	N.S.
Cirrhosis Death Rate		
Total (z185)	.37	.01
Males* (z185)	.33	.01
Females* (z185)	.41	.01
Malignant Neoplasms		
of the Resp. System		
Total (t91r)	.18	N.S.
Males (t314r)	.12	N.S.
Females (t315r)	.49	.001
Suicide		
Total (t391r)	.52	.001
Males (t394r)	.47	.001
Females (t395r)	.60	.001

* Sex differences for cirrhosis are based on white population only.

Table 5-3   Correlation of State Stress Index (tX15) with Six Indicators of Maladaptive Behavior.

correlations are presented for total state population and for each sex separately.[1] Theoretically, stress could have a substantially different effect for men and women for several reasons. The two sexes may be affected by different types and numbers of stressful events, even while sharing the same environment. The same events may have a different meaning and impact on men and on women. The sexes probably differ in their coping mechanisms and in their capacity to use social support to buffer the effects of stressful events (McCormack, 1982). Finally, men and women may differ in the particular form of maladaptive behavior they adopt in response to stress, such as mental distress, physical symptoms, violent and other antisocial behavior, or alcoholism.

The correlations in Table 5–3 are almost all in the direction expected by stress theory. This applies to both correlations for total population and for males and females separately. The higher the level of social stress characteristic of a state, the more common is maladaptive behavior. The major exception is found for deaths due to industrial accidents in which the correlations approach zero ($r = $ .05; .05 and .04). The majority of correlations in the table are significant to at least the .05 level.

Sex Differences. Each of the correlations in Table 5–1 is greater for women than for men but usually by only a small amount. However, the sex difference is especially pronounced for suicide, where the correlation with stress for males is .47 and for females .60; and for lung cancer, where the correlation is .49 for women compared to an insignificant r of .12 for men. This latter finding is consistent with a sociological examination of smoking norms and behavior by Markle and Troyer (1979). They report a rapid recent decline in smoking among males but not among females. They attribute the persistence of female smoking in part to the stress and tension associated with their fuller participation in the labor market.

Net and Interactive Effects of Stress on Maladaptive Behavior

All Accidental Deaths. Section A of Table 5–4 summarizes the regression analysis carried out to test the hypothesis that the higher the level of social stress, the greater the probability of accidental death. The independent variables are the State Stress Index, interaction terms for the five buffer variables, and five control variables (see Chapter 3 for an explanation of the buffer and control variables).

The first two rows of section A show that there is both a strong relationship between the State Stress Index and the rate of accidental deaths and also a significant interaction with the Index of Mental Health Professional Support (see Chapter 3 for a description of this index). The first row shows that when such support is low, there is a strong relationship between the stressfulness of life in states and the overall rate of accidental deaths. For every increase of one point in the State Stress Index, there is an average increase of 1.38 accidental deaths per 100,000, and this relationship is significant at the .001 level. When the state is *above* the median in the number of mental health professionals available, the

Independent Variable	Regression Coefficient	t	p<

A. ALL ACCIDENTAL DEATHS (t151r)
Multiple R squared =.81

State Stress Index:
| When Mental Health Support is Low | 1.38 | 8.46 | .001 |
| When Mental Health Support is High | 1.12 | 4.70* | .001 |

Control Variables:
% Population 15-24 (p5r2)	4.60	5.00	.001
% Population Metropolitan (v206)	-.26	4.73	.001
% Population Black (v750)	-.33	2.07	.05

B. MOTOR VEHICLE DEATHS (t156r)
Multiple R squared =.74

State Stress Index:
| When Pub. Assist. Support is Low | .57 | 5.28 | .001 |
| When Pub. Assist. Support is High | .50 | * | |

Control Variables:
% Population 15-24 (p5r2)	2.29	3.85	.001
% Population Metropolitan (v206)	-.11	3.03	.01
% Population Black (v750)	-.31	3.0	.01

Buffering Variables:
| Mental Health Professionals (xmhp) | -4.59 | 2.49 | .05 |

C. INDUSTRIAL ACCIDENT DEATHS (t161r)
Multiple R squared = .65

| State Stress Index (tx15) | .06 | 3.16 | .01 |

Control Variables:
| % Population 15-24 (p5r2) | .26 | 2.53 | .05 |
| % Population Metropolitan (v206) | -.03 | 4.63 | .001 |

Buffering Variables:
| Mental Health Professionals (xmhp) | -.99 | 3.27 | .01 |

* t = 2.10 (p<.05) for the significance of the difference between the Stress-Motor vehicle deaths relationship when public assistance is low (as given in the previous row) versus the Stress-Motor vehicle deaths relationship when public assistance is high (this row). See footnote to Table 4-7 for further explanation and the regression equation.

Table 5-4   Net And Interactive Effects State Stress And Deaths From Accidents Per 100,000 Population (N=50 States).

link between stress and accidents is still strong but weaker than when a state has few mental health professionals. Thus, there is a significant interaction of stress with the extent to which professional mental health support is available in each state. The effects of stress appear to be mitigated by the availability of mental health professionals in the community in the way expected when it was decided to include this variable in the model.

The first of the control variables in section A of Table 5–4 shows that the percentage of young persons in a state's population is positively related to the accident rate, with all other variables in the equation controlled. For every 1 percent addition to a state's population 15–24, there is an average increase of 4.6 accidents per 100,000 population. This association is not surprising since accidents account for more than one-half of all deaths in the 15–24 age group (Boggs, 1982). The next two control variables, Percent Metro and Percent Black, operate in the opposite direction to age. States with larger percentages of their population metropolitan and states with larger black populations have significantly fewer accidents per 100,000.

Motor Vehicle Deaths. State stress is also related to the motor vehicle death rate as shown in section B of Table 5–4. The relationship between stress and motor vehicle accident deaths is affected by a significant interaction with the level of public assistance support (see Chapter 3 for a description of this variable). When public assistance support is low, there is a stronger relationship between stress and motor vehicle accidents than when public assistance support is higher. This result could be interpreted as generally consistent with the buffering hypothesis. We consider public assistance support as one indicator of community integration—that is, as a measure of a community's concern for all of its citizens. Such integration appears to mediate the effects of stress on the motor vehicle accident death rate.

Three of the control variables are significant. Again, the youthfulness of the population, independent of other variables, is associated with higher rates of motor vehicle accident deaths. Metropolitan population is oppositely related to the death rate for motor vehicle accidents. This finding is consistent with Boggs (1982), who reports that auto fatalities tend to occur disproportionately on rural roads. The percentage of blacks in a state's population is also oppositely related to motor vehicle deaths. Finally, one of the buffering variables, the presence of mental health professionals, has a major effect on the motor vehicle accident rate. States above the median in the number of mental health professionals per 100,000 have between 4 and 5 fewer motor vehicle accident deaths per 100,000 than states with fewer mental health personnel.

These findings for states are consistent with research on life events and accidents at the individual level. One study reported 52 percent of a fatal accident group experienced interpersonal and financial stressors prior to the accident in comparison to only 18 percent of a nonaccident control group (Selzer, 1969). Another study reported that life changes and current subjective stress are significantly related to traffic accidents and are better predictors of such accidents than demographic or personality variables (Selzer and Vinokeur, 1974).

It is easy to lose sight of the fact that our data refer only to associations and are not necessarily evidence of causal relationships and causal direction. Both Boggs (1982) and Palmer (1981:98) question the usual assumptions concerning the link between stress and motor vehicle accidents—that is, stress leads people to expose themselves to hazardous situations, which results in accidents for some. They suggest that much of the data on the subject are compatible with the opposite causal connection—that is, that people engage in hazardous behavior in order to increase their stress level. According to this reasoning, drivers may take risks deliberately to raise their tension levels and to increase the intensity of their experience such as fear and excitement.

In the current study the causal direction is not completely ambiguous. We use the aggregated life events for the year *preceding* the year of the dependent variables—in this case motor vehicle accidents. Many of the life events involved in the State Stress Index (disasters such as fires and floods, employment cutbacks, etc.) are beyond the control of the individuals affected, and several of the most plausible alternative connections between the variables are statistically controlled in the equations.

Industrial Accidents Death Rate. The simple correlations in Table 5–3 showed that the industrial accident death rate was the only one of the six maladaptive behaviors not significantly correlated with state stress. However, the regression analysis in Table 5–4 shows that after other variables are controlled, industrial accidents are in fact related significantly. The regression coefficient of .06 indicates that for each increase of one unit in the State Stress

Index, there is an average increase of .06 deaths by motor vehicle accident per 100,000 population ($t = 3.16$; $p < .01$).

Industrial accidents are also associated with two of the control variables, Youthful Populations and Percent Metro. The regression coefficient of .26 indicates that for every increase of 1 percent in the population 15–24, there is an average increase of one-quarter of an industrial death per 100,000 population ($t = 2.53$; $p < .05$) or, converting this to whole numbers, each increase of 4 percent in the youthful population is associated with an increase of one industrial death. In addition, for each 1 percent increase in metropolitan population, there is a corresponding decrease of $-.03$ deaths from industrial accidents per 100,000 population ($t = 4.63$; $p < .001$).

One of the buffering variables, Mental Health Professional Support, also appears to have a direct effect on industrial accidents. States above the median in the number of mental health professionals relative to population have on average one fewer death from industrial accidents per 100,000 than states below the median in that regard.

The link between increased stress and industrial accidents is supported by Catalano's (1979) study of the effects of economic expansion on manufacturing accidents. He reports that disabling accidents increase during the month that new workers are added but do not remain at that level. He cites the combination of environmental and individual factors affected by economic expansion, including the various life events that require new adaptation on the part of new and continuing workers (longer hours, adjustment to new workers, changes in the work environment, etc.). Our findings thus appear to be consistent with Catalano's findings on industrial accidents.

Cirrhosis. Sociological theories explaining variation in levels of alcoholism between populations have been influenced substantially by the early work of Robert Bales (1946). The first of Bales's three major propositions is essentially a stress hypothesis—that is, the rate of alcoholism is positively affected by social-structural factors that produce stress and tension for members of the society. Although the idea that stress is related to alcoholism is widely accepted, this aspect of Bales's theory has not been tested systematically beyond a series of exemplary "case studies" of particular populations or cultures. We argue elsewhere that the lack of a method to systematically compare the relative amount of stress within different societies and groups has heretofore prevented full testing of this and other theories of the consequences of stress on populations (Linsky, Straus, and Colby, 1985).

The availability of the State Stress Index makes it possible to investigate Bales's proposition. It lets us examine the relationship of stress levels in a population to the prevalence of alcohol problems.

Section A of Table 5–5 shows that the death rate for cirrhosis of the liver is significantly related to state stress when all the other variables in the equation are controlled. For each increase of one point in the State Stress Index, there is an average increase of .03 deaths from cirrhosis per million population. Although the prevalence of alcoholism has traditionally been higher among males, our data show that stress increases the rate of alcoholism among both sexes. The regression coefficient for males is 3.38 ($p < .01$) and for females 2.54 ($p < .001$). While women experience lower rates of alcoholism, their rate seems to be as sensitive to the effects of stress as is the case for men.

Linsky, Straus, and Colby (1985) also examined the relation of the State Stress Index to the death rate from alcoholism and alcoholic psychosis and to per capita alcohol consumption. In each case the state stress was correlated significantly with the indicators of alcohol problems once other variables were controlled.

Chronic Stress.   The life events approach to stress upon which the SSI is based emphasizes new demands or important changes in people's life situations that require adaptation. A second approach in the stress literature emphasizes stressful life conditions and situations (Pearlin et al., 1981). The emphasis is on the ongoing or chronic strains or conditions that exact a toll over time, not because of new adjustments required but because of the persistence of noxious or difficult factors in the individual's environment. Although most recent evidence linking social stress to illnesses and other maladaptive behavior has come from the life events approach, that approach is not necessarily the most efficacious for explaining all disorders (Pearlin et al., 1981). The stressors of nineteenth-century Irish society described by Bales (1946) as contributing to alcoholism in Irish men suggest chronic strain (in the Irish case, a prolonged period of status blockage and sexual frustration adherent to young men's roles), rather than life changes. For these reasons, our alcoholism study included

Predictor Variables	Regression Coefficient	t	p<

A. CIRRHOSIS DEATHS[1] (t161r)
Multiple R Squared = .30

State Stress Index (tx15)	3.12	3.19	.01

B. SUICIDE DEATHS[2] (t391r)
Multiple R Squared = .66

State Stress Index:			
When Public Assistance is Low	1.33	8.80	.001
When Public Assistance is High	1.15	*	
Control Variables:			
% Population Black	-.68	4.56	.001

C. MALIGNANT NEOPLASMS OF THE RESPIRATORY SYSTEM[2] (t91r1)
Multiple R Squared = .65

State Stress Index	.50	3.57	.001
Control Variable:			
% Population Age 55 and Over	2.66	8.67	.001

[1] Rate per million population
[2] Rate per hundred thousand population
* t = 3.79 (p<.001) for the significance of the difference between the Stress–Suicide relationship when public assistance is low (as given in the previous row) versus the Stress–Suicide relationship when public assistance is high (this row). See footnote to Table 4-7 for further explanation and the regression equation.

Table 5-5 Net and Interactive Effects of State Stress and Deaths From Cirrhosis, Suicide and Malignant Neoplasms of the Respiratory System.

measures of chronic social stress that have previously been employed in epidemiological research on suicide, chronic disease, and mental illness.

We employed an abbreviated version of Gibbs and Martin's "Measure of Status Integration" (1964), which purportedly measures the amount of structurally induced role conflict in populations. As a second measure of chronic stress at the state level, we employed an Index of Relative Opportunities (Linsky, 1969), which purportedly measures structural blockage to upward mobility. Both of these measures of chronic stress were found to be correlated with each of the three indicators of alcohol problems that were employed. Thus, no matter which way we measured stress, and no matter which indicator of alcohol problems we used, the findings confirmed the hypothesis that stress is related to alcoholism (Linsky, Straus, and Colby, 1985).

Suicide.   Several of the dependent variables considered in this chapter, such as alcoholism, accidents, and excessive smoking, have elements of self-destructive behavior. Suicide is, of course, the most extreme form of self-destructive behavior. As a manifestation of individual pathology, suicide has attracted the interest of psychologists and psychiatrists for many decades. However, it is also a social phenomenon, and the study of the rates of suicide for different societies and social groups needs to be studied from this perspective as well.

The interconnectedness of suicide with other social phenomena has been a central focus of research since Durkheim's pioneering study of European suicide rates at the close of the nineteenth century (Durkheim, 1951). Durkheim focused on the extent to which individuals were firmly tied to others and to their society as the major explanatory variable. However, he also focused on a second explanation. He argued that when social, cultural, and economic changes occurred too rapidly to be assimilated, the result was a condition of normlessness or anomie, which in turn was linked to rising suicide rates. That condition of externally induced changes in people's lives is not unlike our own focus stemming from the stressful life events tradition—that is, the focus on excessive demands for adaptation to new conditions as the central cause of stress.

At the individual level, recent life events have been implicated in attempted suicides. Paykel et al. (1975) report that suicide attempters experienced four times as many events in comparison with a control group drawn from the general population in the six months prior to the attempt. Life events also have been linked at the individual level with depression (Paykel et al., 1969) and depressive symptomatology (Warheit, 1979). Depressive disorders share some of the same psychodynamic components as suicides in as much as both are presumed to represent aggression turned inward upon the self, and depressed patients are at high risk of suicide (Arieti, 1959).

The findings for American states in section B of Table 5–5 are consistent with the theories and empirical research just cited. They show that state stress, with all other variables in the equation controlled, is significantly related to the suicide rate, and that there is a significant interaction for states with public assistance support. In states that are below the median in public assistance support level, there is on average an increase of 1.33 suicides per 100,000 for every one-point increase in the State Stress Index (Table 5–5, section B). For states *above* the median in public assistance generosity, the regression coefficient is reduced to 1.15. Thus, when public assistance is high, stress is less strongly linked to suicide than is the case in states that are less generous in this regard. We interpret public assistance levels as one measure of social integration—that is, as an indicator of the community's concern for all its members. In this case such integration significantly moderates the effect of stress on suicide.

Only one of the control variables, Percent Black, is significantly related to suicide rates. States with proportionately larger black populations have significantly lower suicide rates. This negative correlation is probably a reflection of the lower average suicide rates among black populations that exists on a national basis (Public Health Service, 1980).

Malignant Neoplasms of the Respiratory System. The final measure of maladjustive behavior is the death rate for malignant neoplasms of the respiratory system. Such deaths are attributed substantially to heavy smoking (Public Health Service, 1964). Smoking behavior could be considered maladaptive in the sense that the link between smoking and illness has been well established and publicized in the ten-year period preceding the reference year of this study (Markel, 1979).

The simple correlations reported in Table 5–1 indicated a positive association between state stress and malignant neoplasms of the respiratory system for the total population and each sex separately. However, only the correlation for females (.49) reached the significance level ($p < .001$). The regression analysis in Table 5–3, which reports the net and interactive effects, indicates that after all other variables in the equation are controlled, stress and respiratory cancer are significantly associated for both males and females. The regression coefficient of .50 (section C of Table 5–3) indicates that there is an average increase of one death per 100,000 population for every two-point increase in the State Stress Index. One of the control variables, Percent Population Age 55 and Over, is also significantly related to the rate of respiratory cancer.

A separate study of stress and smoking in the United States (Linsky, Colby, and Straus, 1986b) examined the relation of stressful events or acute stress (as measured by the SSI) and stressful conditions or chronic stress (as measured by Gibbs and Martin's Measure of Status Integration) to smoking. Preliminary findings from that research indicate that both stressful events and ongoing stressful conditions for states are significantly correlated with smoking, and that smoking in turn is linked to high death rates for respiratory cancer. Those findings hold for two different types of measures of smoking (based on self-reported survey findings and sales tax on cigarettes). The findings also hold with several other variables controlled and for both male and female cancer death rates separately.

The findings for stress, smoking, and respiratory cancer parallel the findings for stress, drinking, and cirrhosis death rates reported above. In both cases, it is health-related behavior (unhealthy activity) that links stress to fatal disease. Most research on the stress-illness connection has relied on either a "direct physiological" or "psychological" model of the process rather than on the "health behavior" model just discussed. In the direct physiological arousal model, stressors appear to operate directly on the physical organism of the individual, resulting in disease-generating processes at a preconscious level (Holmes and Rahe, 1967; Selye, 1966). In the psychological or cognitive model, various psychological processes such as cognitive psychological appraisal, perceived threat, psychological discomfort, and anxiety are seen as mediating the stress-disease relationship (Lazarus, 1966).

The findings just presented for alcohol and smoking suggest that the "health behavior" model of the stress-disease process should receive more attention.

Summary for Maladaptive Behavior

The relationship of state stress to six indicators of maladaptive behavior has been examined in preceding sections of the chapter. The correlation analysis revealed that the more frequently stressful events occur in a state, the higher the rate of each of the six maladaptive behaviors. Except for the death rates for industrial accidents and lung cancer, the correlations are statistically significant. These correlations hold for both males and females separately. However, for reasons to be suggested later, the relationship seems to be stronger for women.

When multiple regresion was used to examine the net and

interactive effects of stress on maladaptive behaviors, we found that once other important explanatory variables are controlled, *stress is significantly related to all six of the indicators of maladaptive behaviors*, including both deaths from industrial accidents and lung cancer. Thus, when a more adequately specified causal model is employed, all six of the maladaptive behavior patterns examined in the section are associated with state stress. The multiple R^2's ranged from .30 to .80, indicating that some of the most important explanatory variables are included in the equation. However, none of the potentially important control variables (Percent Metro, Percent Below the Poverty Level, Percent Black, and Age of Population), nor any of the five buffer variables (Family Integration Index, Percent with Four or More Years of High School, Concentration of Mental Health Professionals, Percent Adults Voting, and Public Assistance Generosity), are consistently related to the maladaptive behaviors. Only the variable of state stress is consistently related.

In addition to the "main effects" for stress, there is a significant interaction of state stress with the level of professional support on the total accidental death rate, and of state stress with public assistance generosity on both motor vehicle death rates and suicide death rates. Each of the three interactions is consistent with the "buffer" theory. That is, the buffer variables lessened the effect of state stress on accidential deaths, motor vehicle deaths, and suicide.

Stress and Disease

Stress in general, and stressful life events in particular, have been linked to the onset of illness by several decades of research at the individual level. This section of the chapter examines whether the concentration of such life events in certain states contributes to higher rates of certain, presumably "stress-related" diseases in those same states.

The *Vital Statistics of the United States* lists mortality according to 281 separate causes of death. For both theoretical and practical reasons, we selected eleven causes of death for this research. These include several diseases that have been linked to stressors through either clinical or statistical studies of individuals. Psychogenic factors are believed to play either a direct role or to be strong contributing factors in the onset of these disorders. This includes deaths from perforated ulcers and from asthmatic attacks (Wolf and Goodell, 1968).

We also included four sub-categories of heart and circulatory diseases. They are ischemic heart disease, arteriosclerotic heart disease, other heart disease, and cerebrovascular disease. There is a long tradition of research on the relation of heart disease to stress. Friedman and Rosenman (1974), for example, attribute the general increase in heart disease over the last half century as due in part to the stresses of living in an increasingly complex society. The emphasis of most of this research has been on internal sources of stress, such as type A personality (Glass, 1977; Rosenman et al., 1975), as compared with the external sources emphasized in our own study.

A recent focus of research in the physiological response to stress is on the immunological aspects of stress and disease (Bieliauskas, 1982; Maier and Laudenslager, 1985). That research suggests severe stress weakens the immunological competency of individuals, leaving them vulnerable to onset of disease. To test this possibility, we include a number of disorders in which infectious agents are purported to come in contact with a weakened host to produce disease. Included in the study are the following categories: respiratory diseases, pneumonia, infectious and parasitic diseases, and tuberculosis. Immunological factors are believed to play a central role in such diseases.

Table 5–6 summarizes the findings on the relationship between stress and the eleven diseases. Because of the importance of the age factor in disease death rates, the simple correlations shown in Table 5–6 are not very meaningful but are presented for consistency with the previous analyses.

Age is likely to play a dominant role in state-to-state variations in mortality for some diseases, particularly chronic and degenerative types which affect middle- and old-age persons especially. States with older-age populations could have high rates of certain diseases on the basis of their age structure alone, regardless of stress or other factors. For these reasons, the beta coefficients in the second column are more appropriate because they control for age.

Because so many regression analyses were needed to examine the relation of stress to these eleven diseases, to save space, the full regression equations will be presented only when there is a significant relationship between state stress and the disease.

Peptic Ulcers

Ulcers are commonly recognized as a danger of employment in high-pressure environments (Bieliauskas, 1982). The stress-ulcer connection has been well established at the individual level (Brady, 1958; Weiss, 1970, 1972), but the physiological mechanism involved remains ambiguous (Bieliauskas, 1982).

Table 5–6 indicates that state stress is related to peptic ulcer deaths only for the female population ($p < .01$). This relationship is examined in more detail in Table 5–7. The regression coefficient of .12 in section A shows that there is an average increase of approximately one death from ulcers per 100,000 women for every increase of seven points in the State Stress Index. The linkage of stress and ulcers for women and not men may reflect the recent increase in employment outside the home, the recent movement of women into more competitive job situations, and other factors to be discussed later.

Two control variables are also related significantly to the death rate for peptic ulcers (Table 5–7). The Percent Population 55 and Older is significantly and positively related to deaths from peptic ulcers, while the Percent Black is negatively related to the death rate for peptic ulcers.

Asthma

Asthma is a tendency toward bronchial constriction that impedes respiration. Clinical studies have demonstrated that such attacks are likely to follow increases in emotional tension among susceptible persons (Weiner, 1977; Wolf and Goodell, 1968). The beta coefficient in Table 5–6 indicates that the death rate from asthma is associated with residence in high stress states for the total population and for women. The more detailed regression results in Table 5–7 (section B) show that there is also an interaction effect. When public assistance support is low, there is on average an increase of .20 asthma deaths per 100,000 population for every increase of one point on the State Stress Index. When public assistance support is

Cause of Death	Simple Correlations of the State Stress	Beta[1]
Peptic Ulcers		
Total (t386r)	-.33*	.02
Males (t389r)	-.25	.08
Females (t390r)	.14	.48**
Asthma		
Total (t381r)	.02	.61**
Males (t384r)	-.05	.10
Females (t385r)	.29*	.50**
Tuberculosis		
Total (t396r)	.41**	.11
Males (t399r)	.43**	.14
Females (t400r)	.26	.08
Ischemic Heart Disease		
Total (t101r)	-.26	-.03
Males (t322r)	-.23	.05
Females (t323r)	-.27*	-.11
Arterosclerosis		
Total (t116r)	-.37**	.04
Males (t334r)	-.24	.19
Females (t335r)	-.43**	-.05
Cerebro-Vascular Disease		
Total (t111r)	-.11	-.02
Males (t330r)	-.06	.01
Females (t331r)	-.15	-.03
Other Heart Disease		
Total (t106r)	-.07	-.22
Males (t326r)	-.04	-.18
Females (t327r)	-.11	-.41**
Respiratory Disease		
Total (t121r)	-.12	.28***
Males (t338r)	-.09	.31
Females (t339r)	-.17	.14
Pneumonia		
Total (t126r)	-.28*	-.08
Males (t342r)	-.18	.00
Females (t343r)	-.32*	-.15
Infectious And Parasitic Diseases		
Total (t71r)	.28*	-.15
Males (t302r)	.28*	-.11
Females (t303r)	.22	-.14
Leukemia		
Total (t96r)	-.25	-.05
Males (t318r)	-.22	.01
Females (t319r)	-.24	-.06

[1] Each beta is for the regression of a death rate on stress with age and the four other control variables and the five buffer variables included in the equation. See Chapter 3 for a list of the control and buffer variables.

*=p<.05, **=p<.01, ***=p<.001

Table 5-6 Correlation And Regression Of State Stress (tx15) With Mortality Rates For Selected Diseases By Sex (N=50 States).

Independent Variables	Regression Coefficient	t	p<
A. DEATHS FROM PEPTIC ULCERS (FEMALE) (t390r)			
Multiple R Squared = .24			
State Stress Index	.12	3.04	.01
Control Variables:			
% Population Age 55 and Over (p10r2)	.31	3.61	.001
% Population Black (v750)	-.07	2.07	.05
B. DEATHS FROM ASTHMA (TOTAL) (t381r)			
Multiple R Squared = .61			
State Stress Index:			
When Pub. Assist. Support is Low	.20	4.73	.001
When Pub. Assist. Support is High	.17	*	
Control Variables			
% Population 55 and Over (p10r2)	.68	6.62	.001
% Population Black (v750)	-.15	4.33	.001
C. RESPIRATORY DISEASES (TOTAL) (t121r)			
Muliple R Squared = .60			
States Stress Index:			
When Pub. Assist. Support is Low	.34	2.38*	.05
When Pub. Assist. Support is High	.24	2.38	.05
Control Variables:			
% Population Age 55 and Over (p10r2)	2.21	7.08	.001
% Population Black (v750)	-.36	2.84	.01

* t = 2.88 (p<.01) for the significance of the difference between the Stress-Asthma relationship when public assistance is low (as given in the previous row) versus the Stress-Asthma relationship when public assistance is high (this row). See footnote to Table 4-7 for further explanation and the regression equation.

Table 5-7 Net and Interactive Effects of State Stress and Deaths From Selected Diseases.

more adequate, the coefficient decreases to .17 asthma deaths per 100,000 for every increase of one point in the State Stress Index. This difference is significant at the .01 level.

While the number of asthma deaths attributed to state stress level is small, there are very few deaths in total from asthma attacks, and the relationship to stress is also highly significant statistically (.001). In that context, stress-related asthma deaths are important.

Tuberculosis

The correlations for tuberculosis in column 1 of Table 5–6 seem to indicate that state stress is associated with death from tuberculosis. In this case, however, the regression coefficients tell a different story. The regression coefficient in the right-hand column shows that once the effects of other variables are statistically controlled, the original association disappears. The full equation (not shown here) reveals a very strong relationship between percentage of a state population below the poverty level and the death rate for tuberculosis. Poverty level is also correlated directly with the State Stress Index. Thus the zero order or simple correlation between state stress and TB would appear to be spurious. It arises because of the joint relationship of state stress and TB to poverty level.

Heart Disease

Four diseases involving the heart and circulatory system are considered next (ischemic heart disease, arteriosclerotic, cerebrovascular and other heart disease). When other factors are controlled, the only significant beta is between stress and "other heart disease" for females, and that association is in the opposite direction to the theory tested. We have no ready explanation for this negative correlation. But since it is the only significant negative correlation, it may well be a random error. The overall finding of no relationship is consistent with a recent review of the stress and hypertension literature, which concluded that the relationship is unproven (Bieliauskas, 1982). Also, a recent review of stressful life events and coronary heart disease shows that the nature of that relationship is still under debate. Although some studies report a positive relationship, others have failed to replicate this result (Mathews and Glass, 1981).

Many of the studies of psycho-social factors in heart disease have focused on "internal" or psychological sources of stress—that is, the Type A behavior pattern. This pattern includes the personality characteristics of impatience and time urgency, competitive achievement, striving, and aggressiveness and hostility (Mathews and Glass, 1981). Mathews and Glass suggest that it is the interaction between Type A coronary prone behavior and uncontrollable stressful events that results in coronary heart disease for some. Our research design does not allow us to test for that particular hypothesis. It does appear, however, that the stressfulness of the environment alone is not sufficient to explain the distribution of deaths from heart or circulatory diseases across states.

Stress and the Immune System

In this section we consider three disease categories in which immunological weakness may play an important role in onset of death. As noted previously, the relationship between stress and susceptibility to disease resulting from changes in immunological competence is an area of growing interest (Stein, Schiavi, and Comerino, 1976; Elliott and Eisdorfer, 1982). There is considerable evidence from research with animals, and somewhat more tentative findings with regard to humans, on the effects of stress on immunological competence (Bartrop et al., 1977; Rogers, Dubey, and Reich, 1979).

Respiratory Diseases

The beta coefficients in Table 5–6 show that respiratory diseases are significantly related to stress levels for the state population as a whole and for males but not females. The more complete regression analysis in Table 5–7 indicates that there is also an interaction with public assistance. When public assistance support is low, there is an average increase of .34 in deaths from this cause for every increase of one point in the State Stress Index. On the other hand, when public assistance is more adequate, there is an average increase of only .24 deaths per 100,000 population for every unit of the State Stress Index. Thus stress results in fewer deaths from respiratory disease in states with more adequate public assistance support levels than in states that are low in public assistance generosity.

Two control variables are significantly related to the death rate for respiratory disease, the Percent Black and the Percent 55 Years Old and Over. Percent Black is negatively related to respiratory deaths (as is also the case for ulcers and asthma), and we have no explanation to suggest for this. A high proportion of elderly persons in the population is positively related to respiratory disease deaths. These are the same two control variables that are significantly related to the other two diseases (peptic ulcers and asthma) reported in Table 5–7.

Pneumonia

Stress is not significantly related to the death rate for pneumonia. There is, of course, the possibility that a relationship may exist between stress and pneumonia, but that it is obscured by some other variables not in the equation, such as regional factors. For example, the death rate for pneumonia could be higher in the north central and north eastern states because of the cold climate. However, these states are among the least stressful according to the State Stress Index.

Infectious and Parasitic Diseases

There is a small positive correlation between state stress and the death rate for infectious and parasitic diseases as indicated in column 1 of Table 5–6. As in the case of tuberculosis and some of the other causes of death considered in this section, the correlation disappears once the effects of other variables are statistically controlled in the regression analysis (see column of betas). Data from the full regression analysis (not shown) suggest that the simple correlation between state stress and deaths from infectious and parasitic diseases arises because of their mutual relationship to the percentage of the population with incomes below the official poverty level.

Stress and Leukemia

Some early work at the individual level with leukemia and lymphoma patients suggests that "recent significant losses were an important risk factor in the development of those illnesses" (Elliott and Eisdorfer, 1982). Our study found that state stress is unrelated to leukemia, as indicated by the nonsignificant betas in Table 5–6.

Of all the control and mediating variables, only the Percent Population 55 and Over was positively related. The Percent Below the Poverty Level was negatively related to leukemia.

To summarize the findings on the eleven selected causes of death, only three were found to be significantly related to state stress in the predicted direction: asthma, respiratory disease, and peptic ulcers (female only). Some possible reasons for the general lack of relationships of stress to mortality for this set of diseases will be presented later.

Sex Differences

Women appear to be more vulnerable to the effects of stressful environments than are men, judging from the findings from this chapter. In most cases the relationship of stress to maladaptive behaviors and diseases is stronger for women (all accidents, motor vehicle accidents, suicide, cirrhosis, and respiratory cancer). For deaths due to asthma and peptic ulcers, the relationship with stress is significant *only* for females and not for males. Thus women seem to be at greater risk of death from the effects of social stressors than men. The single exception is industrial accidents, where males appear to be the more vulnerable. In that case, the sex differences may be a result of occupational segregation of the sexes, since comparatively few women work in heavy industry or with farm machinery where occupational risks are high.

One explanation for the closer association of maladaptive behavior and disease with stress for women lies in the nature of some of the stressful events included in the SSI. Several of the events relate explicitly to women's family roles (divorces, infant deaths, fetal deaths, abortions, and illegitimate births). Other events, such as recent migration and new housing, which tend to be disruptive of personal ties, could also have a greater impact on women than on men. Residential moves are more frequently made because of husbands' job changes, but wives may bear the brunt of adjustment to the new community. Even economic and job-related stressors such as work stoppages and unemployment, which appear to affect men more than women owing to traditional centrality of work roles for men, may be extremely stressful for women because of the strains that these stressors place on entire families and because of women's special responsibility for the well-being of the family.

We are not suggesting that the stronger relationships between stress and disorders are simply a measurement artifact because of this particular set of stressful events in the SSI. We regard this finding as more significant than that. The items that comprise the

SSI were chosen partly because of the convenience of the available data. More importantly, however, they were chosen because of their inclusion in previous stressful life events scales and because, in our view, such events as moving to a different community, divorce, and job loss represent some of the most stressful experiences possible in American life. The fact that women appear more vulnerable than men to the effects of this group of stressors may be a function of women's particular position within the social structure of American society.

On the Lack of Correlation Between Social Stress and Illness

The absence of a relationship between stress and several of the diseases examined is surprising in view of the consistent relationship between stress and the three other main categories of dependent variables: crimes of violence, property offenses, and maladaptive behaviors. Recall from Chapter 4 and the first half of this chapter that almost all the indicators of violent and non-violent crime and maladaptive behavior are positively related to stressful state environments. Also, a plethora of early studies of individuals found links between stressful events and illnesses. Our findings appear, at least at first glance, to be inconsistent with this body of research. The lack of relationship is also surprising on the grounds that the set of diseases included in this analysis were not randomly selected. Instead, studies of individuals provided grounds to suspect in advance that these diseases are "stress-related." In this section we consider several possible explanations for these unexpected findings.

First, a relationship that is true for individuals is not necessarily true for groups and vice versa. Robinson (1950) pointed this out in his classic critique of ecological correlations several decades ago. Stressful life events in states or communities may not have the same health consequence as when the concentration of such events occurs within the life of an individual. If this is the case, then the results of our study would not necessarily be inconsistent with earlier research on individuals. However, more recent critics of Robinson (Firebaugh, 1978) have been able to demonstrate that only rarely and under very special conditions does a relationship at one level change drastically at another level.

Second, in a review of studies that link life events and illness, Thoits (1981) concludes that the previously well established correlations between undesirable life events and disease may have been inflated artificially due to inclusion of health-related events in the list of stressful events (e.g., going to the hospital, having an accident, etc.). She reports that the life events and physical illness relationship is tenuous. If Thoits's finding is substantially correct, our group-level finding of weak or inconsistent relationships between aggregated stressful events and various illnesses may be consistent with individual data.

A second important conclusion from Thoits's findings is that mental health and illness, in contrast with physical illness, is related to life events even in the absence of health-related events in the life events checklists. We were unable to acquire usable measures of mental health for states, so we cannot make a precise comparison. The closest we were able to come to a measure of the mental health of populations were the measures we labeled as maladaptive behaviors. Such indicators as the suicide rate and the death rate for cirrhosis (our indicator of alcohol problems), while not the same as clinical mental illness, may still be construed as indicators of the poor mental health of populations. These indicators are consistently related to state-to-state differences in stressful life events.

A third possibility is that stressful environments and rates of physical illness are truly correlated for states, but we failed to uncover that relationship because our measurement of the disease process is faulty. The life stress and illness theory should apply most directly to the incidence of *morbidity*—that is, onset of illness. According to the theory, persons exposed to highly stressful social environments should have a higher risk of becoming ill and of contracting new diseases. Incidence rates of *morbidity* are better for testing this theory than are *mortality* rates. However, there are almost no published morbidity rates by state for the various diseases in question. Thus, we had to use mortality as the best "stand in" for the incidence of illness, but this poses a number of problems. For example, mortality rates tend to be smaller than morbidity rates for many disorders. Obviously, not every person who develops an illness dies from that illness. Moreover, there is no way of knowing whether the ratio of mortality to morbidity is constant from one state to another. Therefore, using mortality as an indication of morbidity is highly approximate.

Even for those cases of illness that eventuate in death, there is certain to be a time gap between onset of illness and death. The State Stress Index is based on the rate of stressful life events that occur during the year prior to the incidence rate on the dependent variable. Most studies of the individual level have used lags of from six months to two years, with one year being the most frequent interval (Marshall et al., 1982). Our time frame poses no special problems with stress and violence or crime, where the "incubation period" is short or even with some of the maladaptive disorders such as suicide and accidents, which are highly discrete events and immediate in their effects. However, it becomes much more problematical when dealing with some chronic diseases in which the onset may have occurred several years prior to death. A more adequate test of the theory for such chronic disorders would involve a time series analysis to determine the appropriate latency for each illness.

The time gap between stressor events, initial onset of disease, and death creates a further problem for analysis of chronic disease. Many Americans migrate from one state to another. They may be exposed to high or low levels of stressor events in their state of origin, develop disease, but because of the time lag in the morbidity process, contribute to the death rate in their state of destination rather than the state in which the original exposure occurred (Colby, 1981).

Our research design does not provide information to help decide which of these three explanations accounts for the generally weak relationship between the State Stress Index and illness, but we suspect that all three factors may be operating to some degree.

Summary

This chapter reported on the relationship of the stressfulness of the social environment to a group of disorders that we referred to as maladaptive behaviors and to the death rates for several diseases believed to have some psychogenic basis. Of the eleven diseases examined, only the death rate for three—perforated ulcers, asthma, and respiratory disease—were correlated with our stress measure. It is not completely surprising that we did not find heart and circulatory disease, tuberculosis, and infectious and parasitic diseases to be related to the stressfulness of life in different states in view of the fact that we used mortality rates instead of morbidity and in view of the mixed findings of previous research at the individual level.

However, all six of the indicators of maladaptive behaviors, ranging from the death rate from suicide to indicators of excessive smoking and drinking, were correlated with state-to-state differences in stressful life events, even after a number of important other variables were controlled statistically.

Endnote

1. Separate data by sex are available in this chapter from the *Vital Statistics of the United States*. Breakdown by sex was not possible in the previous chapter on crime because the source for that data was the *Uniform Crime Reports*, which do not provide separate data by sex. However, the seven categories of crimes listed tend to be "male crimes" by far.

Part Three

CONTEXT AND CONCLUSIONS

Chapter 6

THEORIES, LEVELS, AND APPLICATIONS

This final chapter serves several purposes. It deals with a number of remaining conceptual and empirical problems. It explores the question of how and why state-level stress is linked in such an impressive fashion to the rates of crime, violence, and many types of maladaptive behaviors. It examines the relationship between individual and community levels of stress as well as their joint impact on several disorders. It compares the concept and theory of "social stress" with the concept and theory of "social disorganization" as alternative or overlapping explanatory models. It illustrates how the State Stress Index could be used for conducting more intensive study of a particular disorder, in this case alcohol problems, and how the expression of stress may be channeled and shaped by the cultural patterns of a state. It considers some practical applications and implications of the State Stress Index and related research, and finally it discusses some unresolved issues and some possible directions for future research using the State Stress Index.

State and Individual-Level Stress

Relationship Between Levels of Stress

In the first five chapters, we presented abundant evidence that socially structured stress is linked to a great variety of crimes and maladaptive behaviors, but we have not tried to explain why and how they are related. We have not dealt extensively with the mechanisms or intervening processes that link state stress levels to high rates of crime and maladaptive behaviors. This chapter focuses on the how and why of these system-level relationships in two ways. This section of the chapter examines the nature of the relationship between state stress and individual-level stress through a multi-level analysis. The next section includes a discussion of whether the correlations of the State Stress Index with rates of crime and various disorders found in this study can be explained by an older systems-level theory—the theory of social disorganization.

The most prevalent explanations for why stress has a "pathological" impact were developed to account for the relationship at the individual level rather than at the social-system level. These explanations refer to psychological and physiological processes as the intervening variables, such as cognitive appraisal, psychological threat, loss of self-esteem, pituitary-adrenal activity, and changes in immunological competence of individuals. Many of these studies were cited as background for the more macro-level relationships that we are investigating because of the scarcity of research at the social level on the consequences of stress.

The current investigation was not prompted by an interest in the consequences of stress for individuals because that relationship has already been well documented by several hundred earlier studies, covering several decades of research. We were able to take as a given and a starting point that cumulative stressful events are related to a variety of human ills for individuals who experience such stressors (Elliott and Eisdorfer, 1982; Thoits, 1983).

There is an important difference between a system-level variable such as the State Stress Index and the individual-level life events scales. At the individual level, the events all occur to the *same* individual, and it is the cumulative buildup of demands for adaptation that results in the stressful reaction. In the case of the SSI measure, however, we do not know that the events occur in the lives of the same individuals but only that they are occurring in the same social environment. The scores then have somewhat different interpretations and implications.

One possibility is that concentration of many life events in the social system increases the statistical probability of such events occurring in combination with other stressful events for individuals living in that system. In turn, some of those who experience an accumulation of life events may suffer the consequences in the form of disabilities or deviance in the way suggested by the many previous studies of life events at the individual level. The concentration of such individuals in certain areas could result in the correlations we observed at the community level. If this were shown to be the case, no further explanation of why state-to-state differences in stressful events lead to high rates of maladaptive behavior would be necessary, since the linkage would occur through the individual-level mechanisms discussed. That is not the only possibility, however.

A second possibility is that the effect of the stressful life events on individuals who directly experience them could lead to a new level of *changes in the community*. This might occur through some type of contagious transmission of stress from individuals directly affected to other individuals with whom they are socially linked, or by changing the nature of the community itself (Brown, 1981).

Correlation of State Stress Index with Individual Stress Scores

In order to determine which of these two possibilities is correct, we need to investigate first how the two levels of stress are related to each other. Such a cross-level analysis would not be possible if we were limited to the same sources of data used thus far—that is, the census, vital statistics, and other public statistics, since they tell us only about states and regions in the aggregate and not about individuals within those populations. Fortunately, we had available national survey interview data (Straus, Gelles, and Steinmetz, 1980), which included several variables that at least partially paralleled the variables in the current study. That survey included a modified version of the Holmes and Rahe Schedule of Recent Life Experience. From the list of items on the survey, we selected a subset of five events that were most comparable with items in the State Stress Index.[1] These five events were used to compute an "Individual Stress Score" for each of the 2,143 respondents in the survey.

The correlation between the State Stress Index and the Individual Stress Score is − .01. This correlation indicates that the two measures of stressful events are completely independent of one another. Thus, persons with higher Individual Stress Scores are no more likely to reside in high stress states than are individuals with lower Individual Stress Scores.[2] Since these two measures are

uncorrelated but each is correlated separately with some of the
dependent variables (see Straus, 1980b, for correlations for the
individuals in this sample), it seems as though there are two
separate effects operating at different levels. If so, the stress
hypothesis has wide scope—that is, it operates at the level of the
individual and at the level of the group or social system. Neither is
explained in terms of the other.

In the following section we return to the issue of how the
community and individual stress levels together affect the rate of
disorders within the communities.

Combined Effects of Social System Stress and Individual Stress

If *individual* stress as measured by the Individual Stress Score and
social stress as measured by the SSI are independent, as they
appear to be, we still need to know if these two variables interact
with one another in terms of their impact on the dependent
variables of this study. Several possibilities exist for the ways in
which social-system level and individual-level stress could com-
bine in their impact on adjustment. Two alternative models of the
joint impact of the two variables are discussed below: the "double
burden model" and "reference group model."

Double Burden Hypothesis. The most stressed people, according to this hypothesis, are those who both experience a cumulation
of stressful events within their own lives, *and* are living in communities characterized by high rates of stressful events. Such
individuals would be at greater risk for the type of maladaptive
behaviors included in this study, such as alcohol abuse or becoming violent toward other individuals, because of the added stress
coming from two sources. In contrast are those persons whose lives
are characterized by stressful events but who live in more tranquil
surroundings.

Reference Group Hypothesis. This hypothesis is the opposite
of the double burden hypothesis just described. Here, the combination of individuals experiencing a cumulation of stressful events
but living among neighbors with more orderly, tranquil lives is
viewed as *more* stressful. This model suggests that events such as
losing one's job or one's business or getting divorced are that much
more stressful if they occur in communities where those events are
exceptional in comparison with experiencing the same events in
communities that are racked by unemployment, high rates of

divorce, and so forth. It is the nefarious comparison of one's own situation and the more fortunate situations of others that adds to the stress of the situation. It is better to be out of work as part of a mass layoff than to be singled out for dismissal according to this reasoning.

The reference group model also draws empirical support from the literature on "social fit," which suggests that having social characteristics dissimilar to one's neighbors, whether it be age, marital status, or ethnicity to name just a few, is a source of high stress (Carroll, 1979).

Data to Test the Hypothesis. The National Family Violence Survey (Straus, Gelles, and Steinmetz, 1980) includes a number of questions about violent behavior within families. Although these measures are not identical to our statewide indicators of violence based on violent crimes known to the police (homicide, robbery, forcible rape, aggravated assault), they do appear to reflect the same tendency to take aggressive or violent actions against other persons.

The survey also included questions on another dependent variable of the current study—drinking behavior. Respondents in the survey were asked about frequency of drunkenness for themselves and for a spouse. How frequently one gets drunk is not the same as the average consumption of alcohol or the death rate for cirrhosis of the liver, but there seems again to be enough overlap to provide useful comparison.

We also included three health-related variables to provide some parallel with the accident and disease section of the dependent variables. These were the only health-related dependent variables in the National Family Violence Survey and provide only a rough comparison with the health indicators in Chapter 5.

Having parallel data on individuals and states for at least some of the independent and dependent variables allows a type of analysis not usually possible within a single study. With the above data, we were able to look at the combined impact of social-system stress and individual stress on some of the dependent variables.

Results of Contextual Analysis. Table 6–1 presents a multi-level analysis in which the impact of state stress and individual stress on the dependent variables can be assessed. The pattern is a complex one. Here, the 2,143 individuals from the survey are divided into four groups, depending on which of the four state quartiles they reside in (High Stress States, High Medium, Low Medium, and Low Stress States).[3] Then correlations were compu-

State Stress Quartiles	A. Health Related Problems		B. Domestic Violence		C. Alcohol Problems	
	Disease & Injuries Q68	Change inb Family Health Q69	Husb to Wife Violence XC12W	Wife to Husband XC15	Husband Gets Drunk QE6H	Wife Gets Drunk QE6W
High Stress (N=476)	.09*	.23***	.13**	.09*	.12**	.12**
High Medium (N=987)	.11***	.21***	.12***	.10**	.16***	.11***
Low Medium (N=407)	.05	.16***	.14**	.19***	.08	.03
Low Stress (N=246)	.03	.15**	.15**	.26***	.12*	.12*

*p<.05, **p<.01, ***p<.001

Table 6-1 Correlations Between Individual Stress Scale and Indicators of Violence, Alcohol Abuse and Illness for Persons Living in States with High, High Medium and Low Levels of State Stress.

ted between the individual stress score and individual scores on health variables, drinking patterns, and domestic violence.

The correlations in Table 6–1 are low but for the most part statistically significant. However, the more relevant aspect of Table 6–1 is that it enables us to examine the "double burden" and "reference group" theories. Evidence in favor of the double burden theory would be present if the correlations are *higher* in the context of a high stress state. Evidence in favor of the reference group theory would be present if the correlations are *lower* in the high stress states. However, the findings do not fall into any such neat pattern.

Reading down the columns of Table 6–1 reveals that the pattern appears to change with the type of dependent variables under consideration. When Health-Related Problems are considered as dependent variables (section A of Table 6–1), there is support for the "double burden" hypothesis. Individuals experiencing many life events are more prone to health problems if they live in states characterized by high stress levels. On the other hand, individuals who experience many life events but who live in states with a lower State Stress Index are less likely to experience such health problems. This model applies to both health-related measures. The correlations in high stress areas are not very high, but are still significant because the size of the sample is substantial.

The pattern with Domestic Violence in section B of Table 6–1 provides partial support for the alternative theory—the reference group model. For wife-to-husband violence, there is a clear gradient in the size of the correlations between an individual's stress score and violent behavior within families. The correlations increase progressively as one moves from high stress states to low stress states. However, the correlations for husband-to-wife violence do not show a similar increase with the stressfulness of the environment. Ironically, it is males who are much more violent than females and the major perpetrators of domestic violence, but men appear to be less affected than women by the stressfulness of their external environment. The sex difference in vulnerability to external stress fits a pattern of findings from the last chapter on maladaptive behavior and disease. Correlations were present only for women or were higher for women than for men between state stress and the following disorders: heavy smoking (respiratory cancer), alcohol abuse (cirrhosis), perforated ulcers, asthmatic attacks, suicides, and accidents. In that chapter we explained the pattern in terms of women's positions within the social structure, which increases their vulnerability to social stress.

Finally, still a third pattern is shown with regard to alcohol problems. Except for the fact that the correlations are lower in the "Low Medium" stress states, there is essentially no difference between the four groups of states in the size of the correlations. It may be that both the "additive model" and the "reference group model" operate simultaneously and effectively cancel each other.

Overall, the context of the state stress level appears to affect individual stress outcomes with the health-related variables consistent with the "double burden" model and the "reference group/social fit model" consistent with the correlations for violence. However, it should be remembered that we did not have strict equivalency of measures of the state and individual levels, and the resulting findings cannot be considered definitive on these grounds.

On the other hand, the differences in contextual effects for health, alcohol problems, and domestic violence might illustrate the complexity of the relationship between stressors and outcomes. Rather than assuming that the same processes link stress with all types of outcomes, it may well be that separate theories are required for the relationship of stress to different types of dependent variables.

Stressful Life Events and Social Disorganization Theory

In the first chapter we discussed some previous approaches used by others to explain many of the same variables considered in this volume. One of these approaches was the social disorganization theory, which first emerged during the 1920s and has been used widely to guide research explaining the rates of crime and delinquency, mental illness, drug abuse, suicide and alcoholism, sexual deviance, and almost every type of social ill.

Commonality of Social Disorganization and Life Events Theory

At the core of the disorganization theory is the breakdown in the predictability of social life that occurs with rapid social change, the loss of stable relationships, and the loss of secure normative guidelines. These factors lead to maladaptive behavior because individuals are destabilized, and social controls which normally constrain aberrant tendencies fail to operate. The fact that both the social disorganization theory and stressful life events research appear to explain the same set of dependent variables may not be accidental. There is in fact considerable continuity if not convergence between the approaches. This would seem to be the case especially when individual life events are aggregated for social systems as we have done in the present case.

From the social disorganization perspective, society is regarded as an organized system in which the various parts (institutions, norms, values, roles) are integrated and relatively consistent with one another. Social disorganization then arises when the various parts of the society become out of phase with one another (Ogburn, 1922). The system no longer functions well, and the influence of social norms and other controls over individuals or particular groups is weakened. A condition of rapid social change underlies most social disorganization. American society was regarded as particularly vulnerable to social disorganization on this score because it was seen as changing at an historically unprecedented speed.

Change is also a significant element in the stressful life events model. Looked at from the standpoint of the individual actor, it is the need to adjust to new situations, roles, and conditions that results in stress for individuals. This is assumed to occur when the total adjustment required by the demands of the situation exceeds the capacity to respond successfully.

Stressful life events include important entrances and exits to and from life's most important roles. It could be argued that when the rate of such changes within a social system becomes too great, there is a breakdown of predictability in social life and a destabilization of relationships. These are the same conditions that are at the heart of the conditions of social disorganization. Hence change is an important element of both models, although it is regarded from the standpoint of the social system in disorganization theory and from the standpoint of the individual life circumstances in most stressful life events research.

Several of the specific indicators that form our stressful life events scales tie into prominent social disorganization themes. Loss of primary group relationships and primary group controls has been emphasized as an important characteristic or cause of social disorganization (Cooley, 1902). Relevant items in our stress scale include the rate of divorce, which represents loss of one of the most central of all primary groups. Other indicators in the State Stress Index include the rate of new cases of unemployment and dropping out of high school. Both represent a separation of individuals from other important institutions of our society and a loss of important group membership.

The illegitimate birth rate and the rate of abortion included in our stressful events scale also may be interpreted as evidence of a weakness of the hold of moral norms over individuals, again a significant characteristic of social disorganization.

Displacement of persons due to migration (Thomas and Znaniecki, 1927) is another frequently cited theme in the writing of disorganization theorists. They argued that immigrants to the United States lacked mutual understanding with native Americans and could not depend on previous norms and behavior patterns to guide them in new situations, and further had conflicts with their new neighbors. Long-distance migration also has the effect of disrupting personal relationships, depriving the migrants of important sources of support. Others, such as Malzburg and Lee (1956), argued that migrants within the United States suffer many of the same problems as do longer-distance migrants.

The most relevant indicator from the State Stress Index in this line is the number of recent migrants to a state (the percentage of the population 14 and over living in a state five years or less). Housing starts (new units authorized per 100,000 population) also reflect the rapid growth of communities. Many of the states ranking high on the State Stress Index are states that have been the target of large numbers of recent migrants.

There are other elements of commonality. Disasters such as floods, fires, hurricanes, and explosions are included in the State Stress Index because they disrupt social organization as a result of the mass displacement of people from their homes, the sudden interruption of normal services and commerce, threats to the safety of the population, and disruption of communication. Such conditions create at least short-term disorganization.

Other factors included in the SSI, such as a high rate of business failures, work stoppages, personal bankruptcies, mortgage foreclosures, and the rate of new welfare recipients, represent malfunctioning and dislocation of the economic system. Likewise, infant and fetal deaths represent the malfunctioning of the health care system.

Many of the life events, looked at from the standpoint of their impact on the social system rather than on individuals alone, would result in a set of conditions substantially the same as what these earlier theorists labeled as social disorganization. They saw social disorganization as causally connected to crime rates and to many of the same maladaptive behaviors that we consider in the current study.

There is a further area of convergence between the stressful life events and the social disorganization approaches. Studies investigating the relation between stressful events and physical and mental health have identified certain "buffer" variables that moderate the relationship between stress and illness and other maladaptive behavior. Primary among the buffer variables is "social support," or the extent to which individuals are enmeshed in an ongoing system of close relationships, such as family, kin, friends, neighbors, and so forth (Gore, 1981). Individuals who enjoy well-developed support systems are better able to cope with stressful events and are less likely to suffer consequences from stress than more isolated individuals. Looked at from the community level, the concept of social support is analogous to "social integration" or the degree of "connectedness" between individuals in a community or group. The absence of social integration is a fundamental aspect of the social disorganization approach.

Unique Aspects of Life Events Theory

So far we have indicated areas of commonality between the life events approach and social disorganization theory. However, life events and disorganization theory also differ in at least two important points: the variables intervening between the events and the maladaptive outcomes, and the specificity and operationalization of the theory.

Intervening Processes. The stressful life events theory emphasizes various psychophysiological mechanisms triggered by stress, which eventuate directly in various maladaptive behavior. Sometimes the emphasis is on physiological mechanisms (Bieliauskas, 1982), sometimes psychological, and sometimes psychological leading to physiological changes (Elliott and Eisdorfer, 1982).

Social disorganization theory, on the other hand, although occasionally including the concept of personal disorganization as an individual condition paralleling and resulting from disorganization at the community level (Rubington and Weinberg, 1977), has a different primary focus. The major intervening variable in social disorganization theory is the breakdown of social controls. Under conditions of social disorganization, the hold of community norms over individuals is weakened, either because the norms themselves become weakened or conflicted or because groups are unable to enforce their norms on individuals. It is this breakdown of social control over behavior that leads to increased deviant behavior in the social disorganization approach (Reckless, 1967).

Specificity and Operationalization. A main problem of social disorganization as an explanatory theory is that it is extremely diffuse. Different authors have emphasized different elements, including breakdown of family life, the loss of neighborhood and other primary group ties, the rapid and uneven social change, and consequences of immigration and migration. At the empirical level, social disorganization researchers tend to operationalize disorganization sometimes by one indicator, sometimes by another. This made it difficult to develop cumulative data about causes and consequences of disorganization.

A further problem with the measurement of social disorganization was that the rates of various social problems were sometimes taken as indicators of the presence of social disorganization (e.g., divorce rates, crime rates, etc.). Since these were often the same social problems that were supposed to be explained by disorganization, there was an unfortunate circularity in the approach (Traub and Little, 1975:33–34).

In contrast to the diffuseness and occasional circularity of the social disorganization approach, life events research in general and the State Stress Index in particular are operationalized very specifically. The State Stress Index, for example, utilizes fifteen specific life events, each of which requires major adjustment for those who experience them. The life events approach appears to have distinct advantages in terms of specificity and clear operationalization.

Integration of Social Disorganization and Life Events Theories

In the previous section, we suggested that explaining the findings on the basis of social disorganization theory was not completely satisfactory because of its conceptual diffuseness and lack of a commonly accepted standard for operationalization of that theory.

However, life events theory is also not fully satisfactory for explaining social system relationships because it is a theory focusing on the stress processes within individuals. Since the findings reported in this book deal with group-level variables and group-level measurement of the independent and dependent variables, it seems inconsistent to explain the relationship on the basis of physiological and psychological processes within individuals. However, group-level processes in the social disorganization theory discussed above may help explain some of our findings. These include the breakdown of informal social controls and the destabilization of relationships.

Scores on the State Stress Index signal the extent to which members of the community are entering and exiting from life's major roles and statuses. High rates of such entries and exits could be thought of as a kind of "social churning" condition which disturbs the stability of social relationships, depriving individuals of important social support. Although most of the social support literature is not specific about what particular aspects of social support account for its effects, the aspects often mentioned include the maintenance of self-esteem, availability of material assistance, information and advice in coping with problems, and the importance of informal social control in keeping people on the straight and narrow. Weakened relationships and the absence of social support have been linked repeatedly to disturbances in mental and physical health and to a variety of maladaptive behaviors (Durkheim, 1951; Elliott and Eisdorfer, 1982).

Stressful Life Events and Societal Reaction

So far, we have discussed two types of intervening processes which could account for the link between the State Stress Index and the dependent variables: psychological processes and social disorganization. Still another possible intervening process is the reaction of social control agencies and agents to high rates of stressful events. Catalano and associates found that increased stress may provoke changes in the organization of social control, both formal and informal, eventuating in higher official rates of disorders. These studies of a metropolitan community (Catalano and Dooley, 1977) and a non-metropolitan community (Catalano, Dooley, and Jackson, 1981) suggest that changes in economic cycles uncover *exist-*

ing untreated mental illness, rather than provoke symptoms in normal persons. Those investigators used combinations of survey data and admissions data for mental health facilities and found that, while holding constant the symptom level in the population, changes in economic conditions were significantly related to changes in inpatient and outpatient admissions, with a two- to four-month time lag. This suggests that communities and families experiencing high levels of stress may be less able to tolerate disruptive behavior. Under such conditions, social control agencies may change the way that they recruit cases.

This type of "societal reaction" or labeling theory may be useful in explaining a stress–mental illness connection and possibly some of the types of disorders included in this study. For example, many types of crime rates are known to be impacted by the efficiency of crime reporting systems and the vigor with which certain laws are enforced. If such increased activity by police was a result of community stress levels, then the stress–crime-rate relationship could be explained by this process. On the other hand, this type of explanation does not seem useful for those types of crimes and disorders for which community and agency reactivity is less of a central element in case finding, such as suicides, fatal automobile and other accidents, and certain psychosomatic diseases; and crimes such as homicide, for which police reporting is believed to be fairly complete. Thus societal reaction is a possible explanation for only some of the relationships revealed in this study.

At this point, we are unable to pinpoint with certainty the mechanism or mechanisms that connect the level of stress in a state to aberrant outcomes. One intriguing example is the striking correlation of the State Stress Index with the rate of forcible rapes ($r = .72$) reported in Chapter 4. Perhaps the mounting tensions and frustrations associated with stressful events directly affects the motivations of rapists to rape. Perhaps stress, as suggested for fatal accidents, operate by increasing the vulnerability of the victims through distraction of attention to danger. Perhaps a high rate of the stressful events in the State Stress Index, such as geographic mobility and divorce, weakens the system of external checks which normally keep rape under control. Unfortunately, these are not the types of questions that can be answered from the data at hand. More detailed research is needed, concentrating on the linkage between stress and one dependent variable at a time, since the intervening processes may well be specific to different types of disorders.

Cultural Factors in Shaping the Directions of Stress Outcomes

We began Chapter 1 with a discussion of the ways in which stress is a sociological as well as a psychological issue. One of the important sociological issues of stress research is why people respond to stress in the particular way they do. A sociological perspective suggests that the way people respond to stress has at least as much to do with the culture of their groups as with the personality or motives of the individuals experiencing the stressful events.

An unresolved problem in social stress theory is a lack of specificity in identifying the outcomes of stress. A great many different types of maladaptive behaviors and physical and mental disorders have been linked to stressful social situations and events. But stress theory is largely unable to explain why such stress results in one outcome rather than another. In this research the same State Stress Index was found to be linked to six different types of violent and nonviolent crimes, to suicides, fatal auto and industrial accidents, smoking, alcohol abuse, and some psychosomatic disorders.

The cultural context within which the stress occurs may help to explain the direction of the outcome. Different outcomes, such as suicide, aggression toward others, or psychosomatic reactions, may each be channeled by particular cultural contexts.

Stress, Alcohol Norms, and Alcohol Problems

A series of papers by the current authors with John Colby are among the few studies that have explicitly investigated the interaction of stress and culture in determining the specific outcome of stress, in this case abuse of alcohol (Linsky, Straus, and Colby, 1985; Linsky, Colby, and Straus, 1985, 1986a).

Robert Bales's Theory of Alcoholism. Several decades ago, Robert Bales (1946) formulated a sociological theory explaining society-to-society differences in the rate of alcoholism by the combination of a social structure that produces stress and tension for its members, together with a cultural system that permits or encourages the use of alcohol to release that tension.

The theory has enjoyed wide currency in the sociology of alcoholism but has not been the subject of much systematic empirical investigation. Lack of such research may be due in part to the previous unavailability of an instrument for measuring social stress in a systematic way. We were able to investigate Bales's theory for the United States by means of the State Stress Index and an index we constructed for measuring the normative system surrounding drinking.

To measure the impact of normative systems on any type of behavior it is important to measure norms independently from the actual behavior that is presumably impacted to prevent circularity in the analysis. To do this we developed a Proscriptive Norm Index based on four separate indicators: (1) the percentage of a state's population that is Fundamentalist Protestant or Mormon, (2) the rate of "on-premise" liquor outlets per million population, (3) the degree to which alcohol sales are restricted in hours, or (4) prohibited on Sundays and on other days of the week. On the basis of a state's ranking on the Proscriptive Norm Index, we divided the states into four quartiles, extending from the most proscriptive states on alcohol use to the most permissive. Alcohol problems were measured by three indicators of heavy drinking: average consumption of alcohol, average consumption corrected for tourism, and the death rate for cirrhosis of the liver.

Table 6–2 allows us to answer the question of whether the normative system of a state influences the stress/alcohol problems relationship. If the theory is correct, the State Stress Index should be linked most strongly to alcohol problems in states that are most permissive regarding alcohol use. The correlations support Bales's theory. Stress is most strongly linked to the amount of alcohol consumed and to cirrhosis deaths within the most permissive group of states. For all three indicators of heavy drinking, the correlations with stress are highest, and in each case statistically significant, within the most permissive quartile of states ($r = .56$, .60, and .75). The data provide strong evidence for Bales's theory of alcoholism—that is, it is the combination of socially engendered stress with a normative system encouraging the drinking of alcohol that is most likely to lead to problem drinking.

In addition to their relevance for Bales's theory of alcoholism, the correlations in Table 6–2 also support a more general and a

Indicators of Alcohol Problems	Normative Constraints on Alcohol Use For:			
	Proscriptive States (N=13)	Moderately Proscriptive (N=13)	Moderately Permissive (N=12)	Permissive States (N=12)
Av. Consumption of Alcohol	.26	.38	-.02	.56*
Av. Consumption with Correction for Tourism	.31	.38	-.02	.60*
Death Rate from Cirrhosis	.04	.69**	.40	.75**

*p<.05, **p<.01

Table 6-2   Correlations of State Stress Index With Indicators of Heavy Drinking For Proscriptive, Moderately Proscriptive, Moderately Permissive and Permissive States.

more important proposition—that the outcomes of stress are channeled or directed by the culture of a group toward particular forms of expression. Further research would be useful to examine the impact of other cultural contexts on forms of maladaptive outcomes, but these initial findings regarding alcohol problems are encouraging.

The study also illustrates the power of the State Stress Index, when used in conjunction with other state-based variables to test important sociological theories.

Practical Implications

Location Decisions

Advice to the public about stress focuses largely on how individuals can better deal with stress, how they can manage their lives to avoid it, and how they can cope with it if it occurs. Such an approach sometimes ignores the fact that stress does not occur in a social vacuum. How much stress one is likely to experience depends in part on where one is located within the social structure. A specific example is our finding that some communities are characterized by more stressful events than others. Accordingly, such communities are also at greater risk of violence and property crimes, and higher levels of suicides, fatal accidents, and alcoholism, to name just a few disorders.

Stressful life events and the stressfulness of the social environment might be important factors for companies or families to weigh in making decisions such as relocation, although certainly not the only factors. First, the act of relocation is stressful in itself. Second, if the move is to a more stressful location, there may be an additional risk posed by residence in the new community.

Although this study was restricted to serious crimes and death rates, these are not the only possible outcomes. It is possible that such increased burdens of stress might be debilitating in less extreme ways. For example, stress might hinder family functioning, drain energy from the workplace, and affect the quality of both family life and work performance. Thus a move to a better-paying job in a high stress area might entail hidden costs that offset the economic advantages.

Evaluating Growth

Several of the fastest-growing states in the country such as Nevada, Alaska, Georgia, Washington, California, and Arizona are also among the highest stress states. Thus they offer the paradox of being stressful and attractive at the same time. Fast-growing communities may offer important economic and life-style opportunities that are readily apparent. However, the findings from this research suggest that there are also important costs in the form of stress and its consequences that may not be as readily apparent. Both sets of factors should be weighed seriously in any calculus of the costs and benefits associated with rapid change.

Potential for Needs Assessment

Planning for mental health type services for the victims of stress requires some form of "needs assessment" in terms of where to locate the scarce service resources available to states. In this regard, a Social Stress Index could be a useful instrument in the planning of mental health prevention and treatment programs by helping to pinpoint particularly stressful locales for various types of intervention. However, the State Stress Index would have to be calculated for smaller geographic units, such as counties, state economic areas, or mental health catchment areas for it to be maximally useful. Most of the fifteen indicators used for the State Stress Index are readily available for smaller geographic areas than states (Shambaugh et al., 1979), so that it would not be an insurmountable task for health planning officials to undertake. At present, such "needs assessment" typically takes three forms:

1. Surveys of potential clients through interviews with representative samples of the community to determine the prevalence of various disorders and thereby the need for specific services. Although this method is probably the most accurate form of needs assessment, it is the least frequently used because it is too costly to be justified by local budgets.

2. Surveys of professionals and experts who frequently come in contact with particular problem areas. For example, if a youth-related program is being considered, the survey might include police chiefs, school administrators, clergy, and members of social agencies, etc. The major deficiency in this method is that there may be many cases that are unknown to agencies and community leaders. In some instances, the visible or known cases may represent only the "tip of the iceberg."

3. Application of some prevalence ratio to population based on national estimates (proportional to size of population). For example, if it is estimated that one in twenty American adults has a particular disorder, then local estimates of the number requiring treatment would be derived by taking 5 percent of the local adult population. This method assumes that the local populations are similar to the national population on which the ratio is originally derived. This assumption is highly questionable in some cases because local populations may have very different cultural histories, socioeconomic levels, and be subject to unusual stresses and strains. Moreover, the national estimates of the prevalence of hard-to-measure problems are themselves seriously open to question. For example, Gusfield (1981) argues that national estimates of the number of alcoholics in the population that are used as a basis for public policy should be regarded more as public rhetoric than as scientific fact.

Thus each of these methods is either questionable on methodological grounds or are too costly to be justified by local budgets. The Stress Index approach to needs assessment, in our view, would be more scientifically valid than approaches currently available to local planners and administrators and less costly to carry out than extensive surveys of potential clients.

Future Research on Social Stress

Current plans are to periodically update the State Stress Index. There is usually a delay, ranging from two to five years, in the availability of the type of public statistics on which the State Stress Index and the dependent variables are based, so that complete currency is impossible.

Having the index for two or more time periods will serve several purposes. It would generate data relative to the trends in stressfulness. It would provide the first clear and objective indication of whether American society is becoming increasingly stressful or not. Trends for different states and regions could also be measured. One of our original assumptions was that the relative position of the states was stable, but this would provide an empirical base for testing that assumption overall and pinpoint specific states undergoing changes. Trends in the dependent variable will be examined as well to determine if these trends can be explained by trends in stress for the United States.

The data for additional points in time will allow us to look at various time lags between the occurrence of the stressor events and the outcomes (see Marshall, Funch, and Feather, 1982). Time lags may well vary for different disorders because the processes intervening between stress and outcome may differ. For example, in a more detailed study of the effects of state stress on cirrhosis rates reported elsewhere (Linsky, Straus, and Colby, 1985), we found evidence of a five- to six-year time lag between social stress and increased consumption of alcohol on the one hand, and the death rate for cirrhosis on the other. Such a lag is consistent with current knowledge of the disease process of cirrhosis. On the other hand, one would expect a shorter "incubation period" between stress and outcomes for such disorders as criminal violence and suicide where mounting stress might provide the immediate impulse to the maladaptive behavior.

The availability of more substantial time differences between the independent and dependent variable will also help to determine more clearly the direction of causation between stress and outcomes, since the order of precedence will be much clearer (see Cook and Campbell, 1979; Rogosa, 1980).

One reason why state stress was found uncorrelated with a number of diseases for which there was prior reason to believe there would be a correlation may be our use of mortality data to measure illness. Morbidity data clearly would be preferable. There should be less time lag between stress and morbidity than there would be with stress and mortality. Also, many people contract diseases without dying from them. We used mortality data as our stand-in for morbidity despite these problems because, for most illnesses, it is currently the only data available for states. However, morbidity data are becoming available on a limited number of diseases and health conditions (Centers for Health Promotion and Education, 1984), and we plan to use that data in future analyses.

Contextual analysis, where data on both state and individual levels can be examined within the same research design, was discussed earlier in this chapter. In this study, only a limited contextual analysis was possible because the Violence in America survey from which data on individuals was taken was based on 2,146 cases. This number was sufficient for the original purposes of that study, but was too small to provide reliable data on each state for the contextual analysis. A second Violence in American Families survey with a sample of 6,002 cases has just become available. This will eventually allow us to conduct a more powerful multilevel analysis of individual and group stress.

Conclusion

Our research, like most life events research, focuses on the deleterious consequences of stressful situations. It involves a conception of social stress in terms of environmental demands that exceed the capacity of the individual to adjust or cope successfully—that is, situations of overinvolvement, excessive role demands, and too much change in short periods of time. However, we are not suggesting that such stressful situations should be avoided at all costs; nor are we presenting low stress environments as a kind of utopia. Recall that some of the areas with the lowest scores on the State Stress Index were rural and small town states. Small town life may be unstressful on many of the indicators of our stress index, but may be experienced as personally confining and even oppressive by some because of heavy demands for conformity and the lack of stimulation. There is some evidence that when demands are too little a different kind of stress may be involved that also has deleterious consequences (Jackson and Tessler, 1982; Palmer, 1981).

There is another reason for not assuming that stressful life events are inevitably harmful. Not all personalities are the same, and some people may thrive on higher levels of stress (Jackson and Tessler, 1982; Palmer, 1981). Klausner's (1968) study of sky divers suggests that some people deliberately seek stress because of the psychic rewards associated with challenge and mastery.

Societies and communities may also benefit in some ways from increased levels of stress. Consider the higher levels of morale, increased solidarity, and heightened sense of national purpose that sometimes develop during wartime. Barton's (1969) study of communities in disaster points out positive as well as negative outcomes of such collective stress situations. This includes the spontaneous outpouring of altruism, such as the sharing of housing and other forms of mutual support. Some of this increased solidarity may extend beyond the time frame of the disaster and recovery period. Everything in life, including stress, has its pluses and minuses.

Endnotes

1. The items were: *Got laid off or fired from work; Death of someone I felt close to; Foreclosure of a mortgage or loan; Serious problem with the health or behavior of a family member;* and *Moved to a different neighborhood or town*. This Individual Stress Scale is comparable but not identical in content to the items in the State Stress Index.
2. All 2,143 cases from the Violence in America Survey were used in this correlation. Each case was assigned his or her own score for the Individual Stress Scale and the state of residence score for the State Stress Index. While it was theoretically possible to follow the alternative procedure of using states as units by aggregating Individual Stress Scale scores by state, it was not feasible because of too few cases in several states.
3. States were divided on the basis of the SSI into relatively equal quartiles of twelve and thirteen states. However, since the states vary greatly in population, there are large differences in the number of cases per quartile.

Appendix

REFERENCES TO DATA SOURCES

The identification codes for variables listed under "Var. Name" are those used in the State and Regional Indicators Archive (SRIA). At the time of this writing, the holdings of the SRIA consisted of approximately 12,000 state-level variables. These data are available for public use. An article describing the SRIA (Straus, 1985a), and information on the codebooks, subject index, etc., is available by writing to the Program Assistant, State and Regional Indicators Archive, University of New Hampshire, Durham, New Hampshire, 03824.

The letters following the number part of some variable names indicate that the original variable has been transformed in one of the following ways:

m   Variable contains a missing value which was replaced by estimated value.
l   The variable includes an outlier whose value was adjusted.
r   The source document variable was transformed to a rate.
z   Z or ZP scored version of a variable.

Var.Name	*Label followed by Source Reference*
h262	MD's: Non-fed, other specialties psychiatry 1976
h262r	MD: Other specialty: psychiatry: @100K pop 1976 $= (100*H262)/PP76$ HEALTH RESOURCES STATISTICS, 1977. Health Manpower and Health Facilities, 1976–1977 Edition. Hyattsville, MD: U.S. Department of Health, Education and Welfare.

145

---

p1	Total population, 1K, 1976
p5	Population: 15–19 years old, 1K, 1976
p5r2	% population 15–24 years old, 1976
	$= 100*(P5 + P6/P1)$
p6	Population: 20–24 years old, 1K, 1976
p10	Population: 55–64 years old, 1K, 1976
p10r2	% population 55 years or older, 1976
	$= 100*(p10 + P11/P1)$
p11	Population: 65 years + older, 1K, 1976
p12	Population: 14 yrs + over, 1976
p14	Population: 18 years + over, 1976
p15	Male population: All races, ages, 1976
p95	# in households, 1K, 1976
p97	Heads of households, living alone: Total, 1K, 1976
p97r1z	Persons in household: % living alone, 1976
	$= 100*(P97/P95)$
p107	Primary family household: husband + wife, 1K, 1976
p107r2z	Primary family household: % husband + wife, 1976
	$= 100*(TP3/P107S)$
p107S	# of households
	$= TP3 + TP4$
p108	Primary family household: Male head, no wife present, 1976
p109	Primary family household: Female head, no husband present, 1976
p110	Primary individual household: Male total, 1K, 1976
p112	Primary individual household: Female total, 1K, 1976
p148	Persons 18+ years, # 4 years high school, 1K, 1976
p148r	Persons 18+ years: % with 4 years high school, 1976
	$= 100*P148/P14$
p168	State resident 5 years or less: % of population age 14+
	DEMOGRAPHIC, SOCIAL AND ECONOMIC PROFILE OF THE STATES: SPRING 1976, U.S. Department of Commerce. Bureau the Census, Washington, D.C.: Current Population Reports, 1979, P–20; No.334.

---

pp76	State population, 1K, 1976

---

t46	# of live births, 1K, 1976
	STATISTICAL ABSTRACT OF THE UNITED STATES, 1978. U.S. Department of Commerce. Washington, DC: Social and Economic Statistics Administration.

---

t57	Divorces per 1,000 population, 1976
	STATISTICAL ABSTRACT OF THE UNITED STATES, 1979, Washington, D. C.: Bureau of the Census, p. 84.

---

t58	Work stops, workers involved, 1K, 1976
t58r	Workers involved in work stoppages per 100,000 adults, 1975
	$= (T58/P14)*100$
	STATISTICAL ABSTRACT OF THE UNITED STATES, 1978, Washington, D.C.: Bureau of the Census, p. 432.

---

t64	# Fetal deaths: Total 1976
t64r	Fetal deaths per 1,000 live births, 1976
	$= T64/T46$
	VITAL STATISTICS OF THE UNITED STATES, 1976 Volume II-Mortality. U.S. Department of Health and Human Services, (PHS)80–1101. Hyattsville, MD: National Center of Health Statistics, pp. 3–9.

---

t70	Infant deaths, 1976
t70r	Infant deaths per 1,000 live births, 1976
	$= (T70/T46)$
	VITAL STATISTICS OF THE UNITED STATES, Volume II-Mortality, 1976. U.S. Department of Health and Human Services, (PHS)81–1101. Hyattsville, MD: National Center of Health Statistics, pp. 2: 29–33.

---

	t71r-t161r were computed by dividing the original variables (t71–t161) by the 1976 population, as in the following example: t71r $= (T71/P1)*100$
t71r	Infectious & parasitic dis.: deaths per 100K, 1976 population, 1977
t91r	Malignant neoplasms: resp. system: deaths per 100K, 1976 pop., 1977
t96r	Leukemia: deaths per 100K, 1976 population, 1977
t101r	Ischemic heart disease: deaths per 100K, 1976 population, 1977
t106r	Other heart disease: deaths per 100K, 1976 population, 1977
t111r	Cerebrovascular disease: deaths per 100K, 1976 population, 1977
t116r	Arteriosclerosis: deaths per 100K, 1976 population, 1977
t121r	Respiratory disease: deaths per 100K, 1976 population, 1977
t126r	Pneumonia: deaths per 100K, 1976 population, 1977
	VITAL STATISTICS OF THE UNITED STATES, 1977 Volume II-Mortality. U.S. Department of Health and Human Services, (PHS)81–1101. Washington, DC: U.S. Government Printing Office, 1981, pp. 1: 250–351

t151r   Accidents: deaths per 100K, 1976 population, 1977
             VITAL STATISTICS OF THE UNITED STATES, 1977
             Volume II-Mortality, U.S. Department of Health and
             Human Services, (PHS)81–1101. Hyattsville, MD: Na-
             tional Center of Health Statistics, pp. 2: 29–33.

t156r   Motor vehicle accidents: deaths per 100K, 1976 pop., 1977
             VITAL STATISTICS OF THE UNITED STATES, 1977
             Volume II-Mortality, U.S. Department of Health and Hu-
             man Services, (PHS)81–1101. Hyattsville, MD: National
             Center of Health Statistics, pp. 2: 29–33.

t161r   Industrial accidents: deaths per 100K, 1976 population,
             1977
             VITAL STATISTICS OF THE UNITED STATES, 1981
             Volume II-Mortality, 1977, U.S. Department of Health
             and Human Services, (PHS)81–1101. Hyattsville, MD:
             National Center of Health Statistics, pp. 2: 29–33.

t171   School enrollments: Ninth grade, 1975
t172   School enrollments: Tenth grade, 1975
             FOSTER, BETTAY J., AND JUDI M. CARPENTER,
             1976. Statistics of Public Elementary and Secondary Day
             schools, Fall 1975: Pupils, Staff, Revenues, Expenditures,
             and Salaries. Washington, DC: U.S. Department of
             health, Education, and Welfare. Education Division.
             (Doc.#NCES yy–145).

t181   School enrollments: Eleventh grade, 1977
t182   School enrollments: Twelfth grade, 1977
t182r   High school dropouts per 100,000 population, 1976
             = ((T172 + T171–T181–T182)/P1)*100
             FOSTER, B.J. AND CARPENTER, J.M. Statistics of
             Public Elementary and Secondary Day Schools 1977–78
             School Year (Final). Washington, D.C.: National Center
             for Education Statistics.

t183   Bankruptcy cases commenced 1976
t183r   Bankruptcy cases commenced per 100,000 population, 1976
             = 100*T183/P1
             ADMINISTRATIVE OFFICE OF THE UNITED
             STATES COURTS, 1976 Annual Report of the Director.
             Washington, D.C.: U.S. Government Printing Services,
             1976, pp. 152–153.

t187   Families assisted: Requ nat assistance, 1976

t187r   Families assisted: Req nat asst @100K, 1976 pop, 1976
        $= 100*T187/P1$

t187r2   Disaster assistance to families by Red Cross per 100,000 pop, 1976
        $= T187R + T190R$

t190   Families by Red Cross chapter, 1976

t190r   Families assisted: Red Cross chapter @100K, 1976 pop, 1976
        $= 100*T190/P1$
        AMERICAN NATIONAL RED CROSS Summary of Disaster Services Activities by Area and State, 1975–76. Washington, D.C.: American Red Cross, Disaster Services, 1977.

t191   Disabled worker awards (SSA): Total, 1976

t191r   Disabled worker award SSA @ 100K, 1976 pop, 1976
        $= 100*T191/P1$

t191r2   New welfare recipients per 100,000 population, 1976
        $= T191R + T197R$
        U.S. DEPARTMENT OF HEALTH, EDUCATION AND WELFARE. Public Assistance Statistics. Washington, D.C.: Social Security Administration.

t197   AFDC: New cases: Fourth quarter, 1976
        APPLICATIONS AND CASE DISPOSITION FOR PUBLIC ASSISTANCE, 1977. U.S. Department of Health, Education and Welfare. Washington, DC: U.S. Government Printing Office (DHEW SRS–77–03109).

t199   Mortgage loans service: First quarter, 1976

t200m   % mortgage loans foreclosed: First quarter, 1976

t200r   Mortgage loans foreclosed per 100,000 population, 1976
        $= (((T200M*T199) + (T202M*T201) + (T204M*T203) + (T206M*T205))/P1)*100$

t201   Mortgage loans serviced: Second quarter, 1976

t202m   % mortgage loans foreclosed: Second quarter, 1976

t203   Mortgage loans serviced: Third quarter, 1976

t204m   % mortgage loans foreclosed: Third quarter, 1976

t205   Mortgage loans serviced: Fourth quarter, 1976

t206m   % mortgage loans foreclosed: Fourth quarter, 1976
        MORTGAGE BANKERS ASSOCIATION OF AMERICA National Delinquency Survey, Washington, D.C., 1125 Fifteenth Street, NW.

---

t207	Illegitimate live births: total, 1976
t207r	Illegitimate live births per 1,000 population age 14+, 1976

$$= T207/P12$$

VITAL STATISTICS OF THE UNITED STATES, 1976 Volume I-Natality. 1976 U.S. Department of Health and Human Services, (PHS) 81–1100. Hyattsville, MD: National Center of Health Statistics, p. 172.

t281	Psychologists per 100K population, 1976
t282	Clinical social workers per 100K population, 1976

UNITED STATES DEPARTMENT OF HEALTH, EDUCATION, AND WELFARE, 1980. The Alcohol, Drug Abuse and Mental Health National Data Book. Washington, DC: U.S. Government Printing Office.

---

t302	Inf and parasitic disease: Male deaths, 1977

$$= T72 + T74$$

t302r	Infect. & paras. disease: deaths per 100K, 1976 male population, 1977

$$= 100*T302/P15$$

t303r	Infect. & paras. disease: deaths per 100K, 1976 female pop., 1977
t314r	Malig. neoplasms: resp. system: deaths per 100K, 1976 male pop., 1977
t315r	Malig. neo.: resp. system: deaths per 100K, 1976 female pop., 1977
t318r	Leukemia: deaths per 100K 1976, male population, 1977
t319r	Leukemia: deaths per 100K 1976, female population, 1977
t322r	Ischemic heart disease: deaths per 100K, 1976 male population, 1977
t323r	Ischemic heart disease: deaths per 100K, 1976 female population, 1977
t326r	Other heart disease: deaths per 100K, 1976 male population, 1977
t327r	Other heart disease: deaths per 100K, 1976 female population, 1977
t330r	Cerebrovascular disease: deaths per 100K, 1976 male population, 1977
t331r	Cerebrovascular disease: deaths pr 100K, 1976 female population, 1977
t334r	Arteriosclerosis: deaths per 100K, 1976 male population, 1977
t335r	Arteriosclerosis: deaths per 100K, 1976 female pop., 1977
t338r	Respiratory disease: deaths per 100K, 1976 male population, 1977

t339r   Respiratory disease: deaths per 100K, 1976 female popula-
             tion, 1977

t342r   Pneumonia: deaths per 100K, 1976 male population, 1977

t343r   Pneumonia: deaths per 100K, 1976 female population, 1977
             VITAL STATISTICS OF THE UNITED STATES, 1977
             Volume II-Mortality. U.S. Department of Health and
             Human Services, (PHS)81–1101. Washington, DC: U.S.
             Government Printing Office, pp. 1, 250–351.

t366r   Accidents: deaths per 100K, 1976 male population, 1977

t367r   Accidents: deaths per 100K, 1976 female population, 1977

t370r   Motor vehicle accidents: deaths per 100K male pop., 1977

t371r   Motor vehicle accidents: deaths per 100K female pop., 1977

t374r   Industrial accidents: death per 100K, 1976 male pop., 1977

t375r   Industrial accidents: death per 100K, 1976 female pop.,
             1977

             VITAL STATISTICS OF THE UNITED STATES, 1977
             Volume II-Mortality, 1977, U.S. Department of Health
             and Human Services, (PHS)81–1101. Hyattsville, MD:
             National Center of Health Statistics, p. 1: 264–353

t381r   Asthma: deaths per 100K, 1976 population, 1975–77

t384r   Asthma: deaths per 100K, 1976 male population, 1975–77

t385r   Asthma: deaths per 100K, 1976 female population, 1975–77

t386r   Peptic ulcer: deaths per 100K, 1976 population, 1975–77

t389r   Peptic ulcer: deaths per 100K, 1976 male population, 1975–
             77

t390r   Peptic ulcer: deaths per 100K, 1976 female population,
             1975–77

t391r   Suicide: deaths per 100K, 1976 population, 1975–77

t394r   Suicide: deaths per 100K, 1976 male population, 1975–77

t395r   Suicide: deaths per 100K, 1976 female population, 1975–77
             VITAL STATISTICS OF THE UNITED STATES, 1975,
             1976, and 1977 Volume II-Mortality, U.S. Department of
             Health and Human Services, (PHS)81–1101. Hyattsville,
             MD: National Center of Health Statistics, pp. 1, 257–301

t396r   Tuberculosis: deaths per 100K, 1976 population, 1975–77

t399r   Tuberculosis: deaths per 100K, 1976 male population, 1975–
             77

t400r   Tuberculosis: deaths per 100K 1976 female population,
             1975–77
             VITAL STATISTICS OF THE UNITED STATES, 1975,
             1976, and 1977 Volume II-Mortality, U.S. Department of
             Health and Human Services, (PHS)81–1101. Hyattsville,
             MD: National Center of Health Statistics, Table 1–27.

---

tx15   State stress index 1976–77
              See Chapter 2 for the 15 indicators of stressful events
              which make up the index, and for the method of comput-
              ing the index. The sources for each of the indicators are
              given elswhere in this appendix.

---

tp3   Total primary family households, 1976
              = P107 + P108 + P109

tp4   Total primary individual households, 1976
              = P110 + P112
              DEMOGRAPHIC, SOCIAL AND ECONOMIC PRO-
              FILE OF THE STATES: SPRING 76, 1979. Population
              characteristics, U.S. Department of Commerce. Bureau
              of the Census, Washington, DC: Current Population
              Reports, P–20; No. 334.

v83   Crime: murder, manslaughter, per 100K, 1976
v84   Crime: forcible rape, per 100K, 1976
v85   Crime: robbery, per 100K, 1976
v86   Crime: aggravated assault, per 100K, 1976
v87   Crime: burglary, per 100K, 1976
v88   Crime: larceny, per 100K, 1976
v89   Crime: motor vehicle theft, per 100K, 1976
              STATISTICAL ABSTRACT OF THE UNITED STATES,
              1977, Washington, D.C.: Bureau of the Census, p. 169.

---

v206   Pop: metropolitan as % of state, 1970
              STATISTICAL ABSTRACT OF THE UNITED STATES,
              1977, Washington, D.C.: Bureau of the Census, p. 17.

---

v242zl   Families: % with own child under 18, 1976
              INFORMATION PLEASE ALMANAC, 1979. New York:
              Information Please Publishing., p. 809.

---

v356r   New housing units authorized per 100,000 population, 1976
              STATISTICAL ABSTRACT OF THE UNITED STATES,
              1977, Washington, D.C.: Bureau of the Census, p. 436.

---

v376   Poverty level: % persons below, 1975
              STATISTICAL ABSTRACT OF THE UNITED STATES,
              1977, Washington, D.C.: Bureau of the Census, p. 458.

---

v382r   Business failures per 1 million population, 1976
              THE WORLD ALMANAC AND BOOK OF FACTS
              1978 New York: Newspaper Enterprise, 1978.

---

v452r   Unemployment—initial claims per 100,000 adults, 1976
              STATISTICAL ABSTRACT OF THE UNITED STATES,
              1977, Washington, D.C.: Bureau of the Census, p. 59.

v706	Votes: % voting age population who voted, 1976
	STATISTICAL ABSTRACT OF THE UNITED STATES, 1977 Washington, D.C.: Bureau of the Census, p. 512.

v750	Pop: black % of total, 1975
	STATISTICAL ABSTRACT OF THE UNITED STATES Washington, D.C.: Bureau of the Census, 1977, p. 31.

v980	Public assistance: average monthly payment per family, 1976
	STATISTICAL ABSTRACT OF THE UNITED STATES Washington, D.C.: Bureau of the Census, 1978, p. 359.

xinf3	Family integration index, 1976
	$= (V242ZL - P97R1Z + P107R2Z)/3$

xmhp	Index of mental health professionals, 1976
	$= T281 + T282 + H262R$

z120r1	Abortions per 100,000 population, 1977
	ALAN GUTTMACHER INSTITUTE Data from xerox copies of computer output provided to Susan Frankel by Alan Guttmacher Institute, 1981.

z138	Deaths from alcic cirrhosis: wh ml 1975–77
z139	Deaths from alcic cirrhosis: wh fm 1975–77
z140	Deaths from alcic cirrhosis: nw ml 1975–77
z141	Deaths from alcic cirrhosis: nw fm 1975–77
z142	Deaths from unspec cirrhosis: wh ml 1975–77
z143	Deaths from unspec cirrhosis: wh fm 1975–77
z144	Deaths from unspec cirrhosis: nw ml 1975–77
z145	Deaths from unspec cirrhosis: wh fm 1975–77
z146	Deaths from other cirrhosis:wh ml 1975–77
z147	Deaths from other cirrhosis:wh fm 1975–77
z148	Deaths from other cirrhosis:nw ml 1975–77
	z149
	Deaths from other cirrhosis:nw fm 1975–77
	Hyman, Merton H., Marilyn A. Zimmerman, Carol Gurioli, and Alice Helrich, 1980. DRINKERS, DRINKING AND ALCOHOL-RELATED MORTALITY AND HOSPITALIZATION: A STATISTICAL COMPENDIUM. New Brunswick, N.J.: Center of Alcohol Studies.

z185	Total cirrhosis deaths per 1M 1975–77
	$= ((Z138 + Z139 + Z140 + Z141 + Z142 + Z143 + Z144 + Z145 + Z146 + Z147 + Z148 + Z149)/(P12*3)*1000)$

REFERENCES

ANGELL, ROBERT C. (1951). "The Computation of Indexes of Moral Integration." Reprinted from "The Moral Integration of American Cities," *American Journal of Sociology,* vol. LVII, No. 1, Part 2 (July):123–126. In Paul F. Larzarsfeld and Morris Rosenberg (eds.), *The Language of Social Research.* Glencoe, Ill.: The Free Press, 1955.

ARIETI, SILVANO (1959). "Manic Depressive Psychosis." Chapter 22 in S. Arieti (ed.), *American Handbook of Psychiatry,* vol. 2. New York: Basic Books, 419–454.

BALES, R. F. (1946). "Cultural Differences in Rates of Alcoholism." *Quarterly Journal for the Study of Alcohol* 6:480–499.

BARON, LARRY, and MURRAY A. STRAUS (1986). "Rape and Its Relation to Social Disorganization, Pornography, and Sexual Inequality in the United States." Paper presented at the International Congress on Rape, Tel Aviv, Israel, April 1986.

BARTROP, R. W., L. LAZURAS, E. LUCHHURST, L. G. KILCH, and R. PENNY (1977). "Depressed Lymphocyte Function after Bereavement." Lancet 2:834–836.

BARTON, ALLEN (1969). *Communities in Disaster: A Sociological Analysis of Collective Stress Situations.* Garden City, N.Y.: Doubleday.

BATESON, G., D. JACKSON, and J. WEAKLAND (1963). "A Note on the Double Bind–1962." *Family Process* 2:34–51.

BIELIAUSKAS, LINAS A. (1982). *Stress and Its Relationship to Health and Illness.* Boulder, Colo.: Westview Press.

BOGGS, RICHARD A. (1982). "Stress-Seeking and Accidents." National Conference on Social Stress Research. University of New Hampshire (October).

BRADY, J. (1958). "Ulcers in Executives and Monkeys." *Scientific American,* 199:362–404.

BRANTINGHAM, PAUL, and PATRICIA BRANTINGHAM (1984). *Patterns in Crime.* New York: Macmillan.

BRENNER, M. HARVEY (1973). *Mental Illness and the Economy.* Cambridge, Mass.: Harvard University Press.

BRENNER, M. HARVEY (1976). "The Impact of Social and Industrial Changes on Psychopathology: A View of Stress from the Standpoint of Macrosocietal Trends." In L. Levi (ed.), *Society, Stress, and Disease.* Oxford: University Press.

BRENNER, M. HARVEY (1980a). "Industrialization and Economic Growth: Estimates of Their Effects on the Health of Populations." Chpt. 2 in M. Harvey Brenner, Anne Mooney, and Thomas J. Nagy (eds.), *Assessing the Contributions of the Social Sciences to Health*. AAAS Selected Symposia Series 26. Washington, D.C.: Westview Press.

BRENNER, M. HARVEY (1980b). "The Influence of Economic Stress on Criminal Aggression." Pp. 143–160 in Martin Molof (ed.), *Colloquiem on Stress and Crime*, vol. II, The Mitre Corporation, 1980.

BROWN, G. W. (1974). "Meaning, Measurement, and Stress of Life Events." In B. S. Dohrenwend and B. P. Dohrenwend (eds.), *Stressful Life Events: Their Nature and Effects*. New York: Wiley.

BROWN, G. W. and T. HARRIS (1978). *Social Origins of Depression: A Study of Psychiatric Disorder in Women*. London, England: Tavistock.

BROWN, ROGER L. (1981). "Economic Downturns and Depression: A Disaggregated Analysis." Paper presented at the Society for the Study of Social Problems, 31st Annual Meeting, August.

BUREAU OF THE CENSUS (1980). *Social Indicators III*. Washington, D.C.: U.S. Government Printing Office.

CAMPBELL, DONALD T. and DONALD W. FISKE (1959). "Convergent and Discriminant Validation by the Multitrait-Multimethod Matrix." *Psychological Bulletin* 56:81–105.

CANNON, W. B. (1963). *Wisdom of the Body*. New York: Norton.

CARROLL, JOSEPH C. (1979). "Social Fit and the Development of Deviant Behavior and Mental Illness." Ph.D. diss., University of New Hampshire, Durham, N.H.

CATALANO, RALPH (1979). "Health Costs of Economic Expansion: The Case of Manufacturing Accident Injuries." *The American Journal of Public Health* 69 (August):789–794.

CATALANO, RALPH and C. D. DOOLEY (1977). "Economic Predictors of Depressed Mood and Stressful Life Events in a Metropolitan Community." *Journal of Health and Social Behavior* 18:292–307.

CATALANO, RALPH, DAVID DOOLEY, and ROBERT JACKSON (1981). "Economic Predictors of Admissions to Mental Health Facilities in a Non-Metropolitan Community." Paper presented at the 76th Annual Meeting of the American Sociological Association, August.

CENTERS FOR HEALTH PROMOTION AND EDUCATION, PUBLIC HEALTH SERVICE (1984). *Behavioral Risk Factor Surveillance, 1981–1985*, vol. 3.3: 1ss–3ss.

CHAMBLISS, WILLIAM J. and M. F. STEELE (1966). "Status Integration and Suicide: An Appraisal." *American Sociological Review* 31 (August):524–532.

CLOWARD R. A. and L. E. OHLIN (1960). *Delinquency and Opportunity: A Theory of Delinquent Gangs*. Glencoe, Ill.: The Free Press.

COBB, S. (1976). "Social Support as a Moderator of Life Stress." *Psychosomatic Medicine* 38:300–314.

COHEN, A. K. (1955). *Delinquent Boys: The Culture of the Gang*. Glencoe, Ill.: Free Press.

COHEN, STANLEY (1980). *Folk Devils and Moral Panics: The Creation of Mods and Rockers*. New York: St. Martin's Press.

COLBY, JOHN P. JR. (1981). "Social Stress and Hypertension Mortality in the United States," M.A. thesis, University of New Hampshire.

COLEMAN, DIANE H. and MURRAY A. STRAUS (1983). "Alcohol Abuse and Family Violence." Chapter 7 in E. Gottheil et al., *Alcohol, Drug Abuse and Aggression*. Springfield, Ill.: C.C. Thomas.

COOK, THOMAS D. and DONALD T. CAMPBELL (1979). *Quasi-Experimentation: Design and Analysis Issues for Field Studies*. Chicago: Rand McNally.

COOLEY, CHARLES H. (1902). *Human Nature and the Social Order*. New York: Charles Schribner's Sons.

DODGE, DAVID L. and WALTER T. MARTIN (1970). *Social Stress and Chronic Illness: Mortality Patterns in Industrial Society*. Notre Dame, Ind.: University of Notre Dame Press.

DOHRENWEND, B. S. and B. P. DOHRENWEND (1974). *Stressful Life Events: Their Nature and Effects*. New York: Wiley.

DOHRENWEND, B. S., L. KRANOFF, A. R. ASKENASY, and B. P. DOHRENWEND (1978). "Exemplification of a Method for Scaling Life Events: The PERI Life Events Scale." *Journal of Health and Social Behavior* 19 (June):205–229.

DOOLEY, D. and R. CATALANO (1980). "Economic Change as a Cause of Behavioral Disorder." *Psychological Bulletin* 87:450–468.

DURKHEIM, EMILE (1951). *Suicide: A Study in Sociology*, trans. by John A. Spaulding and George Simpson. New York: The Free Press.

ELLIOTT, GLEN R. and CARL EISDORFER (eds.) (1982). *Stress and Human Health: Analysis and Implications of Research*. New York.

EYER, JOSEPH (1977a). "Prosperity as a Cause of Death." *International Journal of Health Services* 7 (1):125–150.

EYER, JOSEPH (1977b). "Does Unemployment Cause the Death Rate Peak in Each Business Cycle: A Multifactor Model of Death Rate Change." *International Journal of Health Services* 7 (4):625–663.

FARIS R. E. L. and H. W. DUNHAM (1939). *Mental Disorders in Urban Areas: An Ecological Study of Schizophrenia and Other Psychoses*. Chicago: University of Chicago Press.

FARRINGTON, KEITH (1980a). "Stress and Family Violence." Chapter 7 in Murray A. Straus and Gerald T. Hotaling (eds.), *The Social Causes of Husband-Wife Violence*. Minneapolis: University of Minnesota Press.

FARRINGTON, KEITH (1980b). "Variation in Pace of Social Life and Its Effects: A Macroscopic Analysis." Unpublished Ph.D. diss., University of New Hampshire.

FARRINGTON, K. and A. LINSKY (1976). "The Scheduling of Personal Crises: Seasonal Changes in the Pace of Social Activities and Helpseeking at Mental Health Clinics." Society for the Study of Social Problems, (August).

FIREBAUGH, GLENN (1978). "Individual Relationships from Aggregated Data." *American Sociological Review* 43 (August):557–572.

FRIED, M. (1964). "Effects of Social Change on Mental Health." *American Journal of Orthopsychiatry* 36:3–28.

FRIEDMAN, M. and ROSENMAN, R. H. (1974). *Type-A Behavior and Your Heart*. New York: Knopf.

FUCHS, VICTOR R. (1974). *Who Shall Live?* New York: Basic Books.

GASTIL, RAYMOND D. (1971). "Homicide and a Regional Culture of Violence." *American Sociological Review* 36:412–427.

GERSTEN, J. C., T. S. LANGNER, J. G. EISENBERG, and L. ORZEK (1974). "Child

Behavior and Life Events: Undesirable Change or Change Per Se." Pages 159–170 in B. S. Dohrenwend and B. P. Dohrenwend (eds.), *Stressful Life Events: Their Nature and Effects*. New York: Wiley.

GIBBS, JACK B. and WALTER R. MARTIN (1964). *Status Integration and Suicide: A Sociological Study*. Eugene, Oregon: University of Oregon Books.

GLASER, DANIEL (1971). "Frontiers and the Ecology of Deviance." Chpt. 2 in *Social Deviance*. Chicago: Markham Publishing.

GLASS, D. C. (1977). "Stress, Behavior Patterns and Coronary Disease." *American Scientist* 65:177–187.

GORE, S. (1978). "The Effects of Social Support in Moderating the Health Consequences of Unemployment." *Journal of Health and Social Behavior* 19:157–165.

GORE, SUSAN (1981). "Stress-Buffering Functions of Social Supports: An Appraisal and Clarification of Research Models." In Barbara S. and Bruce P. Dohrenwend (eds.), *Stressful Life Events and their Contexts*. New York: Prodist, pp. 202–221.

GUSFIELD, JOSEPH R. (1981). *The Culture of Public Problems: Drinking, Driving and the Symbolic Order*. Chicago, Il.: University of Chicago Press.

HACKNEY, SHELDON (1969). "Southern Violence." *American Historical Review* 74:906–925.

HANUSHEK, ERIC A. and JOHN E. JACKSON (1977). *Statistical Methods for Social Scientists*. New York: Academic Press.

HICKS, ALEXANDER, ROGER FRIEDLAND, and EDWIN JOHNSON (1978). "Class, Power and State Policy: The Case of Large Business Corporations, Labor Unions and Governmental Redistribution in the American States." *American Sociological Review* 43 (3):302–315.

HARRIES, KEITH D. (1974). *The Geography of Crime and Justice*. New York: McGraw-Hill.

HOLMES, T. H. and M. MASUDA (1974). "Life Change and Illness Susceptibility." Pages 45–71 in B. S. Dohrenwend and B. P. Dohrenwend (eds.), *Stressful Life Events: Their Nature and Effects*. New York: Wiley.

HOLMES, T. H. and R. H. RAHE (1967). "The Social Readjustment Rating Scale." *Journal of Psychosomatic Research* II:213–218.

HOTALING, G. T., S. G. ATWELL, and A. S. LINSKY (1978). "Adolescent Life Change and Illness: A Comparison of Three Models." *Journal of Youth and Adolescence* 7 (4):393–403.

HUMPHREY, JOHN A. and STUART PALMER (1986). "Stressful Life Events and Criminal Homicide." Omega, forthcoming.

HYMAN, MERTON M., MARILYN A. ZIMMERMANN, CAROL GASIOLI, and ALICE HELRICH (1980). "Drinkers, Drinking and Alcohol Related Mortality and Hospitalizations." Center of Alcohol Studies, Rutgers University, New Brunswick, N.J.

JACKSON, E. F. (1962). "Status Consistency and Symptoms of Stress." *American Sociological Review* 27:469–480.

JACKSON, E. F. and P. J. BURKE (1965). "Status and Symptoms of Stress." *American Sociological Review* 30:556–564.

JACKSON, MARY E. and RICHARD C. TESSLER (1982). "Are Stressful Life Events Always Harmful? A Research Note." Paper presented at the National Conference on Social Stress Research. Durham, N.H.

JACOBS, DAVID and DAVID BRITT (1979). "Inequality and Police Use of Deadly Force: An Empirical Assessment of a Conflict Hypothesis." *Social Problems* 26 (April):403–412.

JAFFEE, DAVID and MURRAY A. STRAUS (n.d.). *Social Indicators and Social Research on American States: A Guide to Methods and Data Sources* (in press).

KAPLAN, HOWARD B. ed. (1983). *Psychosocial Stress: Trends in Theory and Research*. New York: Academic Press.

KASL, S. and S. COBB (1966). "Health Behavior, Ilness Behavior, and Sick Role Behavior: II." *Archives of Environmental Medicine* 12: 531–541.

KESSLER, R. C. (1979). "Stress, Social Status and Psychological Distress." *Health and Social Behavior* 20:259–272.

KLAUSNER, SAMUEL Z. (ed.) (1968). *Why Men Take Chances: Studies in Stress Seeking*. Garden City, N.Y.: Doubleday.

LAZARUS, RICHARD S. (1966). *Psychological Stress and the Coping Process*. New York: McGraw-Hill.

LEVINE, SOL and NORMAN A. SCOTCH (1967). "Toward the Development of Theoretical Models: II." *Milbank Memorial Fund Quarterly* 45 (2):163–174.

LEVINE, SOL and NORMAN A. SCOTCH (1970). *Social Stress*. Chicago: Aldine.

LIN, NAN, WALTER M. ENSEL, RONALD S. SIMEONE, and WEN KUO (1979). "Social Support, Stressful Life Events and Illness: A Model and an Empirical Test." *Journal of Health and Social Behavior* 20:108–119.

LINSKY, A. S. (1969). "Social Structure and Depressive Disorders." *Social Problems* 17:120–131.

LINSKY, ARNOLD S. and MURRAY A. STRAUS (1981). "Social Stress in the United States: Some Preliminary Findings." Paper presented at the annual meeting of the Society for the Study of Social Problems, Toronto, August, 1981.

LINSKY, ARNOLD S., MURRAY A. STRAUS, and JOHN P. COLBY (1985). "Stressful Events, Stressful Conditions, and Alcohol Problems in the United States: A Partial Test of the Bales' Theory of Alcoholism." *Journal of Studies on Alcohol* 46:72–80.

LINSKY, ARNOLD S., JOHN P. COLBY, and MURRAY A. STRAUS (1985). "Social Stress, Normative Constraints, and Alcohol Problems in American States." Paper presented at the annual meeting of the Society for the Study of Social Problems, Washington, D.C., August 24, 1985.

LINSKY, ARNOLD S., JOHN P. COLBY JR., and MURRAY A. STRAUS (1986a). "Drinking Norms and Alcohol Problems in the United States." *Journal of Studies on Alcohol*, September.

LINSKY, ARNOLD S., JOHN P. COLBY JR., and MURRAY A. STRAUS (1986b). "Social Stress, Smoking Behavior and Respiratory Cancer: A Macro-Social Analysis." 2nd National Conference on Social Stress Research, Durham, University of New Hampshire.

LOFTIN, COLIN and ROBERT H. HILL (1974). "Regional Subculture and Homicide: An Examination of the Gastil-Hackney Thesis." *American Sociological Review* 39:714–724.

MALZBURG, B. and E. S. LEE (1956). *Migration and Mental Disease: A Study of First Admissions to Hospitals for Mental Disease, New York, 1939–1941*. New York: The Social Science Research Council.

MAIER, S. F. and M. LAUDENSLAGER (1985). "Stress and Health: Exploring the Links." *Psychology Today* (August):44–49.

MARKLE, GERALD E. and RONALD J. TROYER (1979). "Smoke Gets in Your Eyes: Cigarette Smoking as Deviant Behavior." *Social Problems* 26 (June):611–625.

MARSHALL, JAMES R., DONNA FUNCH, and JOHN N. FEATHER (1982). "The Temporal Distribution of the Effects of Stress on Mental Health." National Conference on Social Stress Research, University of New Hampshire, Durham, N.H.

MASUDA, MINORU, D. L. CUTLER, L. HEIN, and T. H. HOLMES (1978). "Life Events and Prisoners." *General Psychiatry Archives* 7, 35:191–203

MASUDA, M. and T. H. HOLMES (1978). "Life Events: Perceptions and Frequencies." *Psychosomatic Medicine* 40 (May):236–261.

MATHEWS, KAREN A. and GLASS, DAVID C. (1981). "Type-A Behavior, Stressful Life Events and Coronary Heart Disease." Pp. 167–185 in B. S. Dohrenwend and B. P. Dohrenwend (eds.), *Stressful Life Events and their Contexts*. New York: Prodist.

McCORMACK, ARLENE (1982). "Cohesive Personal Networks and Medical Help-Seeking under a Condition of Stress: An Exploratory Study of Gender Differences." National Conference on Social Stress Research. University of New Hampshire.

MECHANIC, D. (1962). *Students Under Stress: A Study in the Social Psychology of Adaptation*. New York: Free Press.

MECHANIC, D. (1974). "Discussion of Research Programs on Relations Between Stressful Life Events and Episodes of Physical Illness." Pages 87–97 in B. S. Dohrenwend and B. P. Dohrenwend (eds.), *Stressful Life Events: Their Nature and Effects*. New York: Wiley.

MECHANIC, D. (1978). *Medical Sociology*, 2nd ed. Glencoe, Ill.: Free Press.

MENZEL, HEBERT (1950). "Comments on Robinson's Ecological Correlations and the Behavior of Individuals." *American Sociological Review* 15:674.

MERTON, ROBERT S. (1957). *Social Theory and Social Structure*, rev. ed. Glencoe, Ill.: Free Press.

MISHLER, ELLIOT G. and NANCY WAXLER (1965). "Family Interaction Processes in Schizophrenia: A Review of Current Theories." *Merrill-Palmer Quarterly* 11:269–315.

MOLOF, MARTIN J., ed. (1980). *Coloquium on Stress and Crime*, volume 2. McLean, Va.: The Mitre Corporation.

MURPHY, H. B. (1959). "Social Change and Mental Health." In *Causes of Mental Disorders*. New York: Milbank Memorial Fund.

NUNNALLY, JIM C. (1978). *Psychometric Theory*, 2nd ed. New York: McGraw-Hill.

NYE, F. IVAN (1958). *Family Relationships and Delinquent Behavior*. New York: Wiley and Sons.

OGBURN, W. F. (1922). *Social Change*. New York: Viking Press.

PALMER, STUART (1981). *Role-Stress: How to Handle Everyday Tension*. Englewood Cliffs, N.J.: Prentice Hall.

PARKER, S. and R. J. KLEINER (1966). *Mental Illness in the Urban Negro Community: A Pointed Inquiry into Goal-Striving and Stress in a Climate of Limited Opportunity*. New York: Free Press.

PARSONS, TALCOT (1954). "Certain Primary Sources and Patterns of Aggression in the Social Structure of the Western World." Chapter 14 (pp. 298–323) in *Essays in Sociological Theory,* rev. ed. Glencoe, Ill.: Free Press.

PAYKEL, E. S., JEROME K. MYERS, M. N. DIENELT, G. KLERMAN, J. J. LINDETHOL, and M. PEPPER (1969). "Life Events and Depression." *Archives of General Psychiatry* 21: 753–760.

PAYKEL, EUGENE S., BRIDGET A. PRUSOFF, and JEROME MYERS (1975). "Suicide Attempts and Recent Life Events: A Controlled Comparison." *Archives of General Psychiatry* 32:327–35.

PEIRCE, NEAL R. and JERRY HAGSTROM (1983). *The Book of America: Inside Fifty States Today.* New York: W. W. Norton.

PEARLIN, L. I., M. A. LIEBERMAN, E. MENAGHAN, and J. T. MULLAN (1981). "The Stress Process." *Journal of Health and Social Behavior* 22:337–356.

PETRICH, J. and CHERYL HART (1980). "Arrest and Life Change Magnitude." Pp. 161–176 in Martin Molot (ed.), *Colloquium on Stress and Crime,* vol. 2. McLean, Va.: The Mitre Corporation.

PHILLIPS, DAVID (1977). "Motor Vehicle Fatalities Increase Just After Publicized Suicide Stories." *Science* 196:1464–1465.

PUBLIC HEALTH SERVICE, DHEW (1964). "Smoking and Health: Research of the Advisory Committee to the Surgeon General of the Public Health Service." Washington, D.C.

PUBLIC HEALTH SERVICE, DHEW (1980). *Vital Statistics of the United States,* 1977, vol. 2, part B. Washington, D.C.

RABKIN, J. G. and E. L. STREUNING (1976). "Life Events, Stress and Illness." *Science,* 194:1013–1020.

RECKLESS, WALTER (1967). *The Crime Problem,* 4th ed. New York: Appleton Century Croft, p.397.

ROBINSON, W. S. (1950). "Ecological Correlations and the Behavior of Individuals." *American Sociological Review* 15 (June):351–357.

ROGERS, M. P., D. DUBEY, and P. REICH (1979). "The Influence of the Psyche and the Brain on Immunity and Disease Susceptibility: A Critical Review." *Psychosomatic Medicine* 41:147–164.

ROGHMANN, K. J. (1972). "Book Review of Social Stress and Chronic Illness." *American Journal of Sociology* 77 (March):1019–1020.

ROGOSA, DAVID (1980). "A Critique of Cross-Lagged Correlation." *Psychological Bulletin* 88 (September):245–258.

ROSENMAN, R. H., R. J. BRAND, C. D. JENKINS, M. FRIEDMAN, R. STRAUS, and M. WURM (1975). "Coronary Heart Disease in the Western Collaborative Group Study: Final Follow-Up Experience of 8 1/2 Years." *Journal of the American Medical Association* 233:872–877.

RUBINGTON, E. and M. WEINBERG (1977). *The Study of Social Problems: Five Perspectives.* New York: Oxford University Press.

SCHLESINGER, LOUIS B. and EUGENE REVITCH (1980). "Stress, Violence and Crime." In I. L. Kutash and L. B. Schlesinger (eds.), *Handbook on Stress and Anxiety.* San Francisco: Jossey-Bass.

SCOTT, ROBERT and ALAN HOWARD (1970). "Models of Stress." Pp. 259–278 in Sol Levine and Norman A. Scotch (eds.), *Social Stress.* Chicago: Aldine.

SELYE, HANS (1966). *The Stress of Life.* New York: McGraw-Hill.

Selye, Hans (1980). "The Stress Concept Today." Pp. 127–142 in Chapter 7 in I. L. Kutash and L. B. Schlesinger (eds.), *Handbook on Stress and Anxiety*. San Francisco: Jossey-Bass.

Selzer, Melvin L. (1969). "Alcoholism, Mental Illness, and Stress in 96 Drivers Causing Fatal Accidents." *Behavioral Science* 14:1–10.

Selzer, Melvin L. and Ameram Vinokeur (1974). "Life Events, Subjective Stress and Traffic Accidents." *American Journal of Psychiatry* 131(August):903–906.

Shambaugh, J. Philip, Harold F. Goldsmith, David J. Jackson, and Beatrice M. Rosen (1979). "The Mental Health Demographic Profile System: A Longitudinal Information System." *Social Indicators Research* 6:215–237.

Shannon, Lyle W. (1954). "The Spatial Distribution of Criminal Offenses by States." *Journal of Criminal Laws, Criminology and Police Science* 45:264–273.

Sharkansky, Ira (1970). *Regionalism in American Politics*. New York: Bobbs-Merrill.

Smith, David M. (1973). *The Geography of Social Well-Being in the United States: An Introduction to Territorial Social Indicators*. New York: McGraw-Hill.

Stack, Steven (1980). "The Effects of Marital Dissolution on Suicide." *Journal of Marriage and the Family* 42 (February):83–92.

Stein, M., R. C. Schiavi and M. Comerino (1976). "Influence of Brain and Behavior on the Immune System." *Science* 191:435–440.

Steinberg, Laurence D., Ralph Catalano and David Dooley (1981). "Economic Antecedents of Child Abuse and Neglect." *Child Development* 52:975–985.

Straus, Jacqueline H. and Murray A. Straus (1953). "Suicide, Homicide and Social Structure in Ceylon." *American Journal of Sociology* 58 (March):461–469. Reprinted in Neil J. Smelser and William T. Smelser, *Personality and Social System*, 2nd ed. New York: Wiley, 1970, pp. 647–656.

Straus, Murray A. (n.d.). "The ZP Scale: A Percentaged Z Score Scale." In Murray A. Straus, *Indexing and Scaling for Social Science Research with SPSS*. Book in Preparation. Mimeographed copy available on request.

Straus, Murray A. (1979). "Measuring Intrafamily Conflict and Violence: The Conflict Tactics (CT) Scales." *Journal of Marriage and the Family* 41:75–88.

Straus, Murray A. (1980b). "Stress and Physical Child Abuse." *Child Abuse and Neglect* 45:75–88 and in Ray E. Helfer and C. Henry Kempe (eds.), *The Battered Child*, 3rd ed. Chicago: University of Chicago Press.

Straus, Murray A. (1985a). "Social Stress in American States and Regions: An Example of Research Using the State and Regional Indicators Archive." In Robert F. Allen (ed.), *Data Bases in the Humanities and Social Sciences*. Osprey, Fl.: Paradigm Press.

Straus, Murray A. (1985b). "The Validity of U.S. States as Units for Sociological Research." Paper presented at the 1985 meeting of the American Sociological Association.

Straus, Murray A., and Richard J. Gelles (1986). "Societal Change and Change in Family Violence from 1975 to 1985 as Revealed by Two National Surveys." *Journal of Marriage and the Family* (in press).

Straus, Murray A., Richard J. Gelles and Suzanne K. Steinmetz (1980).

Behind Closed Doors: Violence in the American Family. New York: Doubleday/ Anchor.

STRAUS, MURRAY A. and GERALD T. HOTALING (1980). *The Social Causes of Husband-Wife Violence*. Minneapolis: University of Minnesota Press.

STRAUS, MURRAY A. and FUMIE KUMAGAI (n.d.). "An Empirical Comparison of Eleven Methods of Constructing Indexes." Chapter 2 in Murray A. Straus, *Indexing and Scaling for Social Science Research with SPSS* (in press; mimeographed copy available upon request).

SUCHMAN, EDWARD (1970). "Accidents and Social Deviance." *Journal of Health and Social Behavior* 11:4–16.

THEORELL, T. (1974). "Life Events Before and After the Onset of a Premature Myocardial Infaction." Pages 101–117 in B. S. Dohrenwend and B. P. Dohrenwend (eds.), *Stressful Life Events: Their Nature and Effects*. New York: Wiley.

THOITS, PEGGY (1981). "Undesirable Life Events and Distress." *American Sociological Review* 46 (Feb):97–109.

THOITS, PEGGY (1982). "Conceptual, Methodological, and Theoretical Problems in Studying Social Support as a Buffer Against Life Stress." *Journal of Health and Social Behavior* 23:145–158.

THOITS, PEGGY (1983). "Dimensions of Life Events that Influence Psychological Distress." Pages 33–103 in H. B. Kaplan (ed.), *Psychosocial Stress: Trends in Theory and Research*. New York: Academic Press.

THOMAS, W. I. and F. ZNANIECKI (1927). *The Polish Peasant in Europe and America*, 2 vols. New York: Alfred A. Knopf.

TRAUB, STUART H. and CRAIG B. LITTLE (1975). *Theories of Deviance*. Itasca, Ill.: P. E. Peacock.

TROPMAN, JOHN E. (1978). "Charity Climate: Private Welfare in the American States." *Humboldt Journal of Social Relations* 5 (Spring/Summer): 26–53.

TURNER, R. J. (1981). "Experienced Social Support as a Contingency in Emotional Well-Being." *Journal of Health and Social Behavior* 22:357–367.

WARHEIT, GEORGE J. (1979). "Life Events, Coping, Stress and Depression Symptomatology." *American Journal of Psychiatry* 136:4B (April) 502–511.

WECHSLER, HENRY (1961). "Community Growth, Depressive Disorders, and Suicide." *American Journal of Sociology* 67:9–16.

WEINER, H. (1977). *Psychobiology and Human Disease*. New York: Elsevier.

WEISS, J. M. (1970). "Somatic Effects of Predictable and Unpredictable Shocks." *Psychosomatic Medicine*, 32:397–408.

WEISS, J. M. (1972). "Psychological Factors in Stress and Disease." *Scientific American* 226:104–113.

WILLIAMS, ROBIN M., JR. (1970). *American Society: A Sociological Interpretation*, 3rd ed. New York: Alfred A. Knopf.

WOLF, S. and H. GOODELL (1968). *Stress and Disease*. Springfield, Ill.: Charles C. Thomas.

WYNNE, L., I. RYKOFF, JULIANA DAY and S. HISCH (1958). "Pseudo-Mutuality in Family Relatives of Schizophrenics." *Psychology* 21:205–220.

INDEX

165